Australian Birds

PETER SLATER

Steve Parish

PUBLISHING

In loving memory of
Ellen Collis Slater,
1902–1996

Australian Birds

PETER SLATER

A collection of paintings and drawings

Steve Parish

PUBLISHING

The master potter
  seeking perfect pieces, threw
  on the eighth day: birds

Foreword

As I passed by, the eye contact was intense, riveting. I kept walking, but felt compelled to glance back through the lunchtime crowd. The dark, brooding eyes stared into mine, commanding me to return and gaze in fascination. I was spellbound by a fully mature, magnificent, adult Wedge-tailed Eagle. The year was 1975, the place was a bookshop window in Queen Street, Brisbane, and the eagle was a life-sized Slater masterpiece. Beside the painting there were stacks of Slater field guides and a picture of Peter climbing from a tent hide perched precariously some 24 metres above the ground.

Who was this man? I had to know.

Slater birds have been very much a part of my life now for more than fifteen years. By day, I mainly work with photographs of birds – mine, and those of my bird-nut friends, including Peter – but I can barely imagine life without the Slater paintings that adorn the walls of our home. There, the eyes of an assortment of egrets, eagles, falcons, finches, robins and owls follow me daily as I move about.

Birds have always been objects of sheer delight to me. I care little for species or really even for habits. I just love them as living things. What makes Slater birds so special is that they take you where you cannot go with wild birds: their expressions, their colours and textures, their shapes and their intriguing behaviours are all frozen in time, allowing repeated, sometimes organised, viewings.

Peter Slater is a man whose life is one of total dedication and commitment. In fact, I know of few who would carry out their art with such focus. This man is obsessed, and his obsession is an absolute requirement of his art. The act of finding all but two of the birds in this book, let alone getting close enough to observe the contours, the postures, the textures and the colours, are matters of total devotion to the task and subjects. Capturing their very essence in paint – that's another matter.

I take great pride in publishing this book, a book whose evolution, brushstroke by brushstroke, I have watched with enormous pleasure, over many long years.

Steve Parish

Eastern Yellow Robin – field sketch

Contents

White-cheeked Honeyeater

List of Illustrations

Birds of Woodland and Forest

Parrots and Cockatoos

Rainforest Birds

Water Birds

Birds of Prey

Desert Birds

Ground Parrot

Major Mitchell's Cockatoo

Australian Birds

I have only two memories from my first year of life. One is a paddock full of wheat sheaves covered with crows, which I described as "like little old men with their hands behind their backs". The other is a huge log covered with green moss outside the gate to a farm we visited often. I thought it was a giant lizard or dragon and it figured in my dreams for a long time. It was not until I gathered together the paintings for this book that I realised how often mossy logs figure in my work.

Since that first sighting of crows I have been consumed by a visual hunger for birds. There are those, known as "twitchers", who passionately seek out new species to add to their "life-list", but tend to ignore birds they have seen before. I am far from being a twitcher – any bird will do. I can watch one for hours, whether it is common or rare, and not count the time lost, content to absorb the nuances that make each species unique. Some of the things I see turn up, sometimes years later, in paintings or drawings. There is a long queue of increasingly complex images waiting their turn.

As a child my passion was shared between birds and dinosaurs and I treasured a book called *Whirlaway* which featured an ingenious account of the evolution of life. As far as I'm concerned, the greatest scientific theory of our era is the notion that dinosaurs were warm-blooded and that birds are actually dinosaurs.

The earliest known birds, such as the Jurassic fossil *Archaeopteryx*, were basically dinosaurs with feathers. They did not have the anatomy for sustained flight and probably used their feathered wings to glide. The first known flying birds date from early Cretaceous formations, 120 million years ago. Among them is *Nanantius eos*, found on Warra Station near Boulia in far-western Queensland. *Nanantius* was about the size of a shrike-thrush and, although it retained some dinosaur features, its appearance would have been surprisingly modern. The country around Boulia is now desert, but when *Nanantius* was alive it was lush, probably bordering a huge lake or inland sea. Since Australia then was still attached to Antarctica, South America, India and Africa, which together formed Gondwana, it is likely that birds by then existed worldwide. Thus there were birds in Australia long before it became detached from Antarctica and began its slow trek northwards towards Asia.

In that long journey the landscape has undergone many changes, upheavals and inundations, and the birds have changed to cope, some more than others. The basic similarity between ostriches, rheas and emus, which became isolated from each other about 70 million years ago, suggests that they have not altered very much. *Nanantius* and its allies died out, as have many other adaptations that failed. However, a core of birds persisted on this continent and eventually became what we know as essentially Australian birds: lyrebirds, scrub-birds, tree-creepers, bowerbirds, honeyeaters, magpie geese, crows, and so on. Most of these have remained in the Australian region, but some, such as the crows, vireos and barn owls, have spread onto other continents and done well. Reciprocal immigrations from elsewhere have added to the Australian avifauna, and there is now a mix of truly Australian forms with more recent additions whose degree of adaptation to the Australian environment reflects the amount of time spent here. How quickly a new arrival can fit into the environment is shown by Cattle Egrets, which arrived and proliferated within my lifetime. Australia is also a major wintering ground for northern hemisphere wading birds and sub-Antarctic sea birds. Some of our native petrels, dotterels and ducks were probably annual migrants for a long time before opting to stay and breed.

In this book, I have included 100 or so of the 760 birds now occurring in Australia, hoping to illustrate the beauty and diversity of our avifauna. I have painted every Australian species at least three times, and have photographed about half of them, mostly from hides at close range. Each bird becomes my favourite while I'm watching it, but some linger more vividly than others in my memory, so it is from these special birds that I have made my choice.

The first half of my adult life was spent photographing birds and I lived in out-of-the-way places such as the Nullarbor Plain, the Kimberley, the Western Desert and north Queensland to gain access to them. Like most serious bird photographers, I took enormous risks and escaped death or injury many times by seemingly miraculous circumstances. For instance, while photographing a Little Eagle at its nest I used a rope ladder to climb 20 metres (65 feet) to the hide. While I was climbing down after my last session, the chick having left the nest, the ladder broke when I was less than a metre from the ground. It could have broken at any time in the previous month when I was in a much more vulnerable position.

When we moved to north Queensland to live I lost most of my photographs through fungus and moisture. I remember taking a tea-chest full of photos to the rubbish dump, probably the worst moment of my life. Standing there among the rotting cabbages, I decided to put my cameras away and try my hand at painting. Although I had always pottered around with brush and pencil, I found the learning process hard and painful, and I did not start painting birds seriously until about twenty years ago. One of the pictures in this book dates from that time: the Black Grasswren. The rest represent different stages of my artistic development, although they are not in chronological order. On somewhat dubious advice from a gallery that handled my work, I did not date my painting, and I kept no record of when each was done, so I only have a rough idea of which precedes which. Plainly some are better than others, and I like to think there is some progression. The most recent paintings are the Sea-Eagle with fish, Great Egret, Rufous Fantail, Rose-crowned Fruit-Dove, Little Kingfisher diving and Painted Finch.

When I first started, I used gouache, which is an opaque watercolour, but subsequently switched to acrylic and occasionally oils. A painting is first planned as a rough thumbnail sketch, then a rough drawing is done, followed by a pastel sketch to work out the lighting. A final drawing is made, then transferred to paper or canvas. The background is usually painted first, finishing with the bird and some details in the foreground. I have included examples of each of these stages throughout the book. Most of my paintings are derived from observation, but about twenty per cent are based on photographs from my collection, showing birds in positions held too briefly to be imprinted into my memory.

My aims in painting birds are firstly to show the effect of light and shade on form and feathers, and secondly to capture the "look" of the bird. Every species has its own look, even those that are otherwise closely similar, and it is the greatest challenge to the painter to recreate the little quirks of eye, bill and stance that make each species unique. Great artists like Bruno Liljefors, Joseph Crawhall, Raymond Harris-Ching, William T. Cooper, Ian Lewington, George Maclean, Fenwick Lansdowne, Robert Bateman, Peter Trusler and Chris Bacon do it consistently, others less often or not at all. That is not to say that these others do not do beautiful paintings; it is just that their birds often look not quite right. Regardless of this, next to looking at birds, I love best looking at bird paintings, and I never approach a painting censoriously, but rather look for the good things in it. I am particularly interested in the artists who first painted Australian birds – Georg Forster, William Ellis, Thomas Watling, George Raper, John Hunter, "The Port Jackson Painter" (probably Henry Brewer), John Lewin (who arrived in 1800 on the same ship, HMS *Minerva*, as my convict forebear, Thomas Macalister), Ferdinand Bauer, Edward Lear, Thomas Mitchell, Charles Sturt, Elizabeth Gould, Rowena Birkett and Gracius Broinowski.

Outside of bird paintings I enjoy artists like Willem Claesz. Heda, Pieter Claesz, Carel Fabritius and Jean-Baptiste Chardin. For a while in the eighties I was influenced by the Claesz family and painted studies like the cockatoo opposite, the Blue-winged Kookaburra, Wedge-tailed Eagle, Regent Parrot, Yellow Chat and two of the Riflebirds. Apart from that, I have tried to avoid any influences other than the birds themselves. Whether I am successful or not, I hope you find something to appreciate in my pictures and enjoy the anecdotes and historical notes that go with them.

Female Red-tailed Black-Cockatoo

19

Overleaf: Great Egret

Birds of Woodland and Forest

Woodlands and forests represent the largest habitats in Australia frequented by more than half of Australia's birds, so those I have chosen are a small sample only. Honeyeaters are very much in evidence. There are about 65 species and they make up a major part of our avifauna. They are responsible for pollinating many species of trees and plants while taking nectar from flowers with their brush-tipped tongues. The length of the bill indicates roughly the sort of flowers each bird prefers. The nomadic Scarlet Honeyeater, with its long slender bill, favours tubular flowers, such as grevilleas, but also gathers, sometimes in large quarrelsome numbers, in flowering eucalypts and melaleucas.

Some of the prettiest sights I have seen were male fairy-wrens courting with flower petals in their bills, the Red-backed with scarlet petals and the others with white, violet or blue. Generally these males are intruders into other males' territories, and are known as "furglers". The petals are for show only, although I did photograph one male feeding a petal to a nestling. Fairy-wrens and robins feed on insects – fairy-wrens are foliage gleaners, mainly in the understorey, while robins pounce down onto their quarry on the ground. They are often parasitised by cuckoos; the robins mainly by the Brush Cuckoo and fairy-wrens by the Fan-tailed and the smaller bronze-cuckoos. A friend of mine saw a cuckoo take chicks out of a fairy-wren's nest, presumably to induce the birds to build again so that the new nest could be parasitised. Fairy-wrens and robins of one sort or another are to be found virtually wherever one travels in Australia, from rainforest to desert. In the drier woodlands they probably absorb sufficient moisture from insects and morning dew, so do not require access to standing water.

Finches feed mostly on seed and their distribution in drier areas is dictated by the availability of water. The Zebra Finch has developed physiological strategies for conserving water, but still must drink regularly. It is probably Australia's commonest bird, except during prolonged droughts. Some finches have been affected by a variety of factors and are disappearing at an alarming rate. The Red-browed of the east and the Long-tailed of the north are still common, but the Gouldian, Star and Black-throated are no longer seen in their former considerable numbers. Races of the Star and Black-throated are virtually extinct in the southern part of their range and the plight of the Gouldian, so popular in captivity, is cause for concern. The 7000 birds I saw in a trapper's holding cages in 1955 probably exceed the numbers of birds now left in the wild. It is possible to reintroduce captive stocks into the wild, but the main problem, and a very serious one, is ensuring that exotic diseases are eliminated from them first.

Magpies, on the other hand, have proliferated because clearing of forest and woodland has created ideal habitat for them. Some of the quail have done well too, for example the Stubble Quail and Little Button-quail. But others, if not endangered, are at least difficult to find. The Black-breasted Button-quail of the central east coast is regarded as rare, but may be more common in lantana thickets than is suspected, while the Buff-breasted Button-quail of Cape York is one of the least observed Australian birds.

Bee-eaters, White-throated Needletails and Dollarbirds are all common migrants that live on insects taken in flight. The bee-eater favours stinging insects and removes the stings from bees before swallowing them. Swifts, incredibly, can pick out stingless drones from swarms of bees while flying through them at upwards of sixty kilometres an hour. Dollarbirds seem to prefer cicadas – all of the prey brought to nests where I have photographed them consisted of the large noisy cicadas – but on summer evenings when flying ants and termites are swarming, one suddenly sees dozens of Dollarbirds up hawking, their silver wing-spots alight in the afterglow. Spotted Nightjars are much more difficult to watch because they are nocturnal, but they do have a very bright eye-shine in torchlight, so can be followed to see what they are doing, although rather unsatisfactorily. To me their lovely haunting calls off in the distance, usually on a stony ridge, are the best part of sitting around the camp at night, the perfect end to a day birdwatching in woodland.

Fan-tailed Cuckoo

BLUE-FACED HONEYEATER

PLUM-HEADED FINCH

CHESTNUT-CROWNED BABBLER

SQUATTER PIGEON

Female Scarlet Honeyeater

Immature Scarlet Honeyeater

For many years, I maintained a small waterhole in the Moggill State Forest near Brisbane, taking water down each day. Tamest and most numerous of many species coming to drink was the Scarlet Honeyeater. The event clearest in my mind is the occasion when thirteen males alighted on a stick I had placed over the water. I took a photo, but such is the speed of their reflexes that only four birds were still sitting when the shutter fired. In this habitat, they nest early, starting in mid winter, and continuing through October. By September the first modestly-plumaged young ones visit the waterhole. In July the following year, young males begin assuming adult colouring, almost like a slow-motion blush beginning on the forehead and extending down the body.

Inspired by this new livery, they chase each other like live coals through the forest and eventually set up territories by calling from the tops of the tallest trees. Before the Noisy Miners came and drove them away, some nested at our place — the sketch shows a young male on a hybrid Kangaroo Paw in our garden.

Male Scarlet Honeyeater

Eastern Yellow Robin

Another common bird around the waterhole in the Moggill State Forest near our home is the Eastern Yellow Robin, although individuals come to water only late in the day, some when it is almost too dark to see. Occasionally on very hot days they come at other times. Thirteen pairs nest in the seven hectares of surrounding bush, so there is considerable conflict when a thirsty bird tries to make its way through hostile territories to the water. There are not too many places where robins achieve a greater population density, although I wouldn't be surprised if there were more in some parts of the Macpherson Range of south-eastern Queensland. There, the late Roy Wheeler, one of Australia's greatest birdwatchers and most lovable characters, used to get us out of bed not much past midnight to listen to the dawn chorus. The Yellow Robins always started first, some, I swear, at about

3 a.m., and from the degree of answering back and forth there must have been dozens within audible range. Now that Roy has gone, I'm sure they start calling much later.

Yellow Robins occupy a variety of habitats from rainforest to open woodland, where they require at least some understorey for protection. In the darker northern rainforest, they have developed a yellow rump that shows up in the gloom when the tail is raised in characteristic fashion. When hunting, they typically perch sideways on tree trunks and take most of their insect prey on the ground. I have often seen them catch small lizards also. The nest is usually built in a fork and beautifully decorated with hanging strips of lichen and bark. Young birds are streaked grey and brown, but moult within a few months into an immature plumage similar to adults'.

Just after World War II, I attended a Perth boarding school, a place I felt was harsh and repressive. On reflection, I realise that, because of my interest in birds, I enjoyed privileges not permitted to other students, no doubt due to the intercession of my beloved Biology teacher, Mildred Le Souef (later Mrs Manning). On occasional Saturday afternoons, I was allowed to visit the South Perth Zoo, where Milly lived. Every fourth Saturday afternoon I made my way to the museum to attend meetings of the Junior Naturalists Club, run by Lucy and Vincent Serventy. Vin became a great influence in my life, just as he later influenced the Australian conscience as a leader in the conservation movement. On one occasion he told me about an albino Scarlet Robin sharing a farm in the south-west near Boyanup. A friend and I went down to see if we could find it. Vin had written down some directions, but, as his writing is reminiscent of chicken scratchings, we came across the right farm only by sheer accident. The farmer's wife, with considerable pride, led us through the paddocks until we came to a grove of trees where the robin lived. I remember the day was cold and misty, with fine drizzle that enhanced the beauty of the bird when we eventually spotted it. I know now it was not an albino but a leucino. The main difference is that leucinos have normal eyes, while albinos have pink eyes and are virtually blind, so they rarely survive. Also, the robin had lost the melanin pigments from its feathers but not the scarlet – albinos have a total loss of pigment. I have tried to paint it as I remember it, huddled against the cold, as a way of recreating a beautiful creature and saying, "Thank you, Vin".

Male Scarlet Robin

Leucino Scarlet Robin

Female Scarlet Robin

Male Red-capped Robin

31

Rainbow Bee-eater

Rainbow Bee-eater

The first bird I photographed from a hide was a Rainbow Bee-eater at its nest, and I will never forget the excitement of seeing such a beautiful bird so close. The nest was in a vacant paddock across the road from Karrakatta Cemetery near Perth, Western Australia. The site is now occupied by a Salvation Army Retirement Village, and the bee-eaters have moved into the cemetery itself where my father-in-law, Aubrey Moore, has been studying them for many years. Being migrants, they arrive in the second or third week of October and begin digging their burrows in the sandy lawns. They perch on convenient tombstones, and in late afternoon light present as strangely moving a sight as one could see. A few years ago, a fox from King's Park discovered the colony and each season digs down to the nesting chamber at night once the chicks are large. Aubrey has tried to protect the nests with wire mesh, but the colony has dwindled from fifty or more to only a handful. Probably only one fox is responsible, and once it is gone the colony may well recover. But this small tragedy could well be enacted all over the south-west wherever the birds tunnel into sandy soil.

Eastern Star Finch

In 1839, John Gould came across the Star Finch in small numbers on the Namoi River in New South Wales, which was towards the southernmost end of its range. Since then, the eastern race, which ranged from the Namoi to central Queensland, has virtually disappeared and must now rank as one of our rarest birds. It has been recorded as extinct, but I have heard reliable reports of a small flock "somewhere in central Queensland". The northern race is still observed frequently in the north-west, but elsewhere it too is vanishing and may be reduced to critical numbers before the causes of their decline are identified.

When I lived in the east Kimberley, many years ago, northern Star Finches were still common but many were trapped for export. One trapper I came across used a White Goshawk to keep finches away from one waterhole while he trapped at another. By trapping at waterholes he caught virtually all the finches in the vicinity. It is probable that trapping was only one contributing factor to the species'

decline: other reasons could be burning of herbage by pastoralists, changes to the abundance of native grasses, trampling of waterholes by cattle, and introduced diseases. There are considerable numbers of Star Finches in captivity, from which restocking could take place, but there are very few, if any, eastern birds, and this is a real tragedy. Because they are marginally less attractive than northern birds, most have been hybridised to produce "better-looking" birds. Any breeder who has pure eastern birds should be encouraged, as a moral obligation, to isolate them from northern Stars and develop the strain, with the ultimate aim of re-introducing them to their former habitats. There has been a very commendable effort to build up captive numbers of the "Chocolate Diggles", a form of the Black-throated Finch that is almost extinct in the wild.

Northern Star Finch

Red-browed Finch

Gynandromorph Gouldian Finch

Gouldian Finch

In 1955, I came across a bird-trapper in the Kimberley, one of about forty trappers, who invited me to visit his aviaries next time I was in Perth. When I turned up some months later, I was staggered to find he had 7000 Gouldian Finches, trapped in the east Kimberley, ready for export to Holland and England. I can tell you, so many purple breasts in one place was an unbelievable, if depressing sight. Suddenly I noticed one bird in the melee that defied belief – a gynandromorph, the only one I have ever seen, illustrated in the painting above. One side of the bird was female, the other male, and the split down the centre was perfect. For one side of the head to be red, the bird's male parent probably had one red-headed gene and one black-headed gene, while the hen was most likely red-headed. Such a pairing would result in all male progeny being red-headed and half of the females black-headed. Unfortunately, I lost sight of the bird in the confusion of fluttering birds and could not locate it again.

Years later, I checked the Customs figures for Gouldian exports in 1955, and the figure given was about 2000. From this slight evidence, I fear that the number of birds exported until 1960, when an export ban was imposed, was actually many times greater than the figures quoted on Customs manifests. Trapping of Gouldians for Australian consumption persisted until 1982 when it was noticed, with some surprise, that they were becoming rare. The decline has continued since and at the moment the species must be regarded as endangered. Its disappearance has happened so quickly that there is a real possibility it will be the next Australian bird to become extinct in the wild. There are hundreds of thousands in captivity around the world from which restocking could be attempted, but the number of mutations being bred leads one to suspect that pure Gouldians may not be very common.

Long-tailed Finch

The factors causing the decline of the Gouldian Finch, Star Finch and Black-throated Finch do not appear to have affected the Long-tailed Finch so far. Each time I travel to the Top End I find them still in numbers, often drinking and bathing in roadside puddles. In the west Kimberley, birds have yellow bills; east of the Ord River their bills are coral red, forming a beautiful harmony with the chestnut plumage. John Gould noted that a specimen in the British Museum had a tail 135 mm (5¼ inches) long: normally the central tail-feathers measure 80–90 mm. An interesting feature is that captive birds never acquire a tail as long as a wild bird's.

Trappers I encountered in the east Kimberley in the 1950s were not interested in the long-tails there because they had yellow bills; obviously these were not in demand with aviculturists. I suspect some trappers made forays across the border looking for red-billed birds, which they referred to as Heck's

Finch, because several asked me if I knew where any "Heck's" could be found. Various books confuse the races. The yellow-billed race, *acuticauda*, was discovered in 1838 by Benjamin Bynoe, probably in the vicinity of Cape Leveque or the Fitzroy River in the west Kimberley, and it ranges across the Kimberley to the Ord River. Red-billed birds were called *hecki* in 1900 by Otto Heinroth, from examples in the Berlin Zoo that were probably imported from Darwin: they range from about the Western Australia–Northern Territory border to north-western Queensland. It is interesting to note that John Gould received specimens from Darwin but failed to register the difference in bill colour.

[Incidentally, the day after writing the preceding notes, I received a book about the animal artist Wilhelm Kuhnert. Its foreword was written in 1925 by Professor Heck, director of the Berlin Zoo, which solved for me the problem of who the heck he was.]

Chestnut-backed Button-quail

Female Brown Quail

Female Stubble Quail

Buff-breasted Button-quail

Painted Button-quail

Male Brown Quail

Male Stubble Quail

Male Buff-breasted Button-quail   Female Buff-breasted Button-quail

Red-backed Button-quail

Female Black-breasted Button-quail

Female Chestnut-backed Button-quail   Male Chestnut-backed Button-quail

Female Red-backed Button-quail   Male Red-backed Button-quail

Male Painted Button-quail   Female Painted Button-quail

Male Brown Quail (blue phase)   Male Brown Quail (grey phase)   Male Brown Quail (brown phase)

Little Button-quail   Male Black-breasted Button-quail   Plains-wanderer   Female King Quail

Male Black-breasted Button-quail   Female Black-breasted Button-quail   Red-chested Button-quail   Male King Quail

                    Male King Quail   Juvenile King Quail   Female Red-chested Button-quail

Male Little Button-quail   Female Little Button-quail   Female King Quail   Male Red-chested Button-quail

Female Brown Quail   Male Stubble Quail   Female Stubble Quail   Female Plains-wanderer   Male Plains-wanderer

The Superb Fairy-wren was one of the first Australian birds to be painted by a European. Captain Cook's third expedition anchored at Adventure Bay, Tasmania, for four days in January 1777. Surgeon William Anderson collected a number of birds and described them in his journal, among them a male Superb Fairy-wren, which he called the Azure Motacilla, *Motacilla azurea,* believing it to be related to wagtails which have the scientific name *Motacilla.* Assistant Surgeon William Ellis was a fine artist, and he painted four of the birds collected at Adventure Bay, one of them the wren, which he called *Motacilla cyanea* in his own journal which was published in 1782. Anderson died of consumption before the expedition returned home and his journal remained unpublished, so the Superb Fairy-wren bears the name Ellis gave it, *Malurus cyaneus* (Ellis 1782). Because the Fairy-wren is not a wagtail, *Motacilla* has been changed to *Malurus,* of masculine gender, so *cyanea* has taken the masculine form, *cyaneus.*

Other wrens were among the early ornithological paintings – the Red-backed, Variegated and Southern Emu-wrens were among bird pictures by Thomas Watling and others that were collected by Surgeon John White in the period 1788–94. The black and white form of the White-winged Fairy-wren and the Western Grass-wren were illustrated by Jacques Arago, artist aboard the French ship *Uranie* which visited Shark Bay in 1818. Arago lost many of his drawings and specimens, "the fruits of more than three years of fatigue, search and sacrifice", when *Uranie* was wrecked on the homeward voyage.

Variegated Fairy-wren, race *dulcis*

Superb Fairy-wren

In my picture of the Blue-breasted Fairy-wren I have endeavoured to make a stylistic tribute to those early paintings. The other wren I have chosen is the form of the Variegated Fairy-wren found in the Top End of the Northern Territory. A similar bird, but with the female having chestnut feathering around the eye, occurs in the Kimberley west to the Grant Range. At Derby, only 100 kilometres further westwards, the Variegateds, particularly the females, were quite different, being more similar to those found throughout central Australia, and having brown rather than blue backs.

Blue-breasted Fairy-wren

Black Grasswren

The Black Grasswren is one of the few Australian birds that have eluded me so far. I don't feel comfortable painting birds that I haven't seen, but, many years ago when I did this painting, I felt that I was starting to get somewhere. However, a well-known British artist who visited me at the time was very critical of what I was doing, particularly of this painting, so I spent several painful months evaluating my work. I eventually came to the conclusion that, regardless of the criticism, it was best to continue painting birds the way I see them, but not to get too complacent about the results.

I came across the White-throated Grasswren on the escarpment at Waterfall Creek in Kakadu National Park. We spent a day there tramping through the spinifex, sighting all the other special Kakadu birds but not finding any grasswrens. The following morning at dawn I sat on a rocky outcrop overlooking a stretch of spinifex, and, just as the sun hit a rock I was watching, a grasswren skittered onto it, then stood throwing a long shadow, a heart-stopping moment. Soon four more burst from the spinifex, two of them very playful, wrestling on the ground and rolling over and over. They stayed in view for ten minutes, then, as I tried to creep closer, they disappeared in a flash, not to appear again.

Ten minutes is not enough time to imprint a bird onto my brain, so I need to go back, if only to check whether my image captures the grasswren's essence. But it is a bird I feel I could happily spend the rest of my life painting.

Blue-winged Kookaburra

The Kookaburra is probably the best-known Australian bird and could, with justification, be regarded as an antipodean icon. However, it is not native to Western Australia, but was introduced in 1897 by Colonel Le Souef, Director of the South Perth Zoo, and has subsequently flourished. In my younger days in the West, I regarded it as something of a pest, suspecting it of preying on nestling birds. To test this belief and with the help of my friend Ray Garstone, I set up a hide at a nest where the kookaburras had plenty of opportunities of catching young birds. My intention was to take photographs to determine what the kookaburras were feeding to their chicks, possibly confirming our suspicions. The first item that was brought to the nest was a writhing Dugite (a venomous snake) measuring half a metre. In quick succession, grasshoppers, small skinks and a Western Bearded Dragon were fed to the kookaburra chicks. We watched the nest over a period of several weeks without seeing any variation in this diet and without any observation at all of predation on baby birds, even though there were about a dozen clearly visible nests containing nestlings within fifty metres. From this flimsy evidence, including observations at other nests, we concluded that perhaps the kookaburra was not a feral pest after all – but that was before I became interested in reptiles.

Laughing Kookaburra

Australian Magpie: male black-backed, female western, male white-backed

The painting of the magpie (opposite) was based on a bird that regularly visited our back yard and interested me principally because of the uncharacteristic scaly feathers on the back, reminiscent of female birds in Western Australia, on the other side of the continent. I suspect the bird was sired by a white-backed male I recorded at College's Crossing, about ten kilometres from our home. This was a most unusual sighting because the normal range of white-backed magpies is about a thousand kilometres away. All of the magpies in our vicinity are, or should be, black-backed, so I assume that the painting is of a hybrid. I had no idea why a white-backed magpie should occur so far from its expected range until I exhibited the painting with a note about its history. A woman who had, some time earlier, moved to Queensland from South Australia

approached me after the exhibition and told me that she had brought her pet white-backed magpie with her. It eventually disappeared and she feared that it had met with an untimely end. Seeing my painting and the accompanying story I had written, she believed that her bird may have made its way to College's Crossing, although it is fifty kilometres or so from her home, and joined a flock of magpies there, eventually producing the bird I painted. Australian Magpies live in social groups that are aggressively territorial, so it is logical to assume that the tame magpie would probably have had to move a long way before it encountered a group that was prepared to accept it. I haven't seen the white-backed bird for some years, and the hybrid no longer visits us, nor have I seen any others like it, so perhaps it was just an aberration.

Red-backed Kingfisher

The bird we know as the Dollarbird was once called the Broad-billed Roller. Many species of roller have wings with large bluish-white patches that make an eye-catching contrast to the surrounding colourful feathers. Albrecht Durer painted a famous sketch of a European Roller's wing in the sixteenth century. I was not thinking of that great artist when I made this painting, but rather about a painful occurrence in our back yard. The down side of being known to have an interest in ornithology is that one is often given injured birds. Nowadays there are many dedicated people who devote their lives to caring for unfortunate creatures and we refer such injuries to them, but, years ago, we felt obliged to do our best, and rehabilitated about as many avian invalids as succumbed. One I remember was a Dollarbird with a wing too severely mangled to be reset. It became very tame and "talked" to us almost like a member of the family. Each morning it was put outside to get some sun, and had a special branch it liked to sit on. New neighbours moved in next door and the first inkling I had that they owned some dogs was a loud cackling from the Dollarbird. Through the window, I saw two large Samoyeds jumping up trying to grab the bird. Before I could dash outside, one of them seized the poor creature, killed it, dropped it on the ground and slobbered off across the yard with its mate, without a backward glance. I picked up the bird, took it inside, stretched it out on the work-bench and made the painting reproduced opposite. The dogs somehow survived and our new neighbours moved shortly afterwards.

Spotted Nightjar

The White-throated Needletail is one of the largest members of the family of swifts, well-named for they are very fast in the air. The bird I have painted was perhaps not fast enough. We were driving towards Wiseman's Ferry in New South Wales when we entered a gloomy stand of tall eucalypts enclosing the road on each side. I could see a bird flying in panic-mode ahead of a car several hundred metres in front of us. It was flicking from side to side and I thought it was a hobby (a small falcon) looking for a way to escape. Eventually the car ahead overtook it and the desperate bird smacked into the windscreen, tumbling over and over. It was dead before we reached it, and, when I picked it up, I was astonished to find it was a Needletail, a bird of the open skies. I took it home, and, feeling sorry, painted it back in its usual environment.

I don't remember my birthdays as a rule, but one 17th of October was memorable. I needed to draw some particular leaves to finish a painting, so headed due west in my car to the nearest tree of the required species that I knew of. About 50 kilometres the other side of Dalby, Queensland, I started seeing flocks of Needletails. For the next 100 kilometres the flocks persisted at between three and ten kilometre intervals. I found my tree, made the sketches, then headed back home – Needletails were still crossing the road over the hundred-kilometre front. I could

not begin to imagine how many there were, but, assuming there were at least 20 000 and possibly as many as 100 000, I made rough calculations to determine how many insects they consumed. Overseas studies suggest each swift eats between 400 and 3000 insects per day, depending on size. Taking an average of 1000, this wall of swifts must have accounted for between 20 and 100 million insects per day. Squinting between the mashed remains of some they had missed, I went back to concentrating on my driving.

Swifts capture their prey in flight, using the enormous gape as a scoop. Nightjars employ a similar method, but catch their quarry at night, so moths figure largely in their diet. Their gape is even wider than that of the swift, and some, such as the Large-tailed Nightjar of the north-eastern rainforests, have stout bristles on either side of the mouth to extend the size of the scoop. The Spotted Nightjar lacks these bristles, lending credence to the latest research which suggests that the two sorts of nightjars are only distantly related and may belong to separate families. The bird I have painted is also one I picked up dead on the road. Unfortunately, it is a species given to sitting on outback roads at night. It has a particularly bright eye-shine when lit by headlights, so considerate motorists should have plenty of time to avoid the bird.

White-throated Needletail

Parrots and Cockatoos

Parrots and cockatoos are so distinctive that there is no possibility of confusing them with other birds. They do not seem to have any close relatives and are probably of very ancient lineage – the oldest known fossils, dating from 30 million years ago, are modern in appearance, so they may be much older than that. How many species have flourished and died in that time we will never know, but currently in Australia there are fourteen species of cockatoos and thirty-nine parrots, one of which, the Paradise Parrot, may have become extinct in the last fifty years. The Budgerigar, at the other extreme, is one of the commonest Australian birds, both in the wild and in captivity. It has been described as the world's most popular pet, first taken to England in 1840 by John Gould who acquired birds from his brother-in-law, Charles Coxen. Since then, most Australian parrots and cockatoos have been much in demand as cage-birds, and many thousands were exported until a ban was imposed in 1960. Unfortunately, demand has increased and smuggling continues, particularly of the rarer and more showy species.

No matter where one travels in Australia, there are parrots and cockatoos to be found, even in the densest rainforests or most remote deserts. The Princess Parrot is found principally in the western deserts and, like most inland birds, breeds up in good years and declines during droughts. Being nomadic, it is very difficult to find, and sightings are among the most highly prized by birdwatchers. As they are seed-eaters, the arid country parrots need access to water and will fly considerable distances to drink. Some, like Bourke's Parrot, the Scarlet-chested Parrot, the Naretha Bluebonnet and the Night Parrot, conserve water by remaining inactive during the day, and feed either in the cooler hours of morning and evening or at night. The Night Parrot also may chew vegetation to extract water. Thus they probably need to drink less often than other parrots.

Most parrots and cockatoos nest in tree hollows, the exceptions being the Night Parrot and Ground Parrot, which nest on the ground in dense vegetation, and the Rock Parrot, which nests among rocks along the southern coastline. Most birds start incubating their eggs once the clutch is complete so that all hatch at the same time, but cockatoos and parrots begin incubating when the first egg is laid, so hatching is not synchronised. I imagine this is a survival characteristic to cope with the typically Australian interspersing of good years with drought – in times of plenty all the chicks are well fed, but when little is available only the oldest are fed, as they are largest and best able to compete. The Black-Cockatoos lay one or two eggs and almost invariably only one chick survives. It is fed by the adults for an abnormally long time, from six to eight months, so a larger brood would be too much to cope with.

Major Mitchell's Cockatoo

MAJOR MITCHELL'S COCKATOO

RED-TAILED BLACK-COCKATOO

GALAH

GALAH

Major Mitchell's Cockatoo

Thomas Mitchell achieved fame as an explorer of the Australian interior, but is perhaps better remembered through the bird that bears his name, Major Mitchell's Cockatoo. Contrary to popular belief, he was not the discoverer of the species, and it was originally called Leadbeater's Cockatoo, after a London dealer in natural history specimens. However, Mitchell did make the first, and one of the most beautiful, illustrations of it. On July 10, 1836, he noted in his diary:

"The eye of the eagle and the rich crest of the cockatoo of the desert, could not be preserved as dead specimens, and were too fine to be omitted among the sketches I endeavoured to snatch from Nature."

He also noted that "the pink-coloured wings and glowing crest might have embellished the air of a more voluptuous region".

To see the painting he made from his sketches, one must open the pages of his book, *Three Expeditions into the Interior of Australia*, published in 1838. Had Benjamin Leadbeater been able to paint, no doubt we would still be calling the bird Leadbeater's Cockatoo. I suppose he can't complain — Leadbeater's Possum was named after his son.

Major Mitchell's Cockatoo

If Galahs were rare they would be seen for what they are - extremely lovely birds. But they are common enough to be considered pests in some places, while their noisy screeching and crazy antics have resulted in their very name entering our language as a term for a stupid person. Some of the biggest flocks I have seen, in excess of ten thousand birds, were in South Australia. In flight, wheeling in unison like a cloud changing from pink to grey, they are a magnificent sight. Farmers don't necessarily regard them with the same admiration, and studies have been undertaken to examine their problems.

We once stayed with an ornithologist who was experimenting with ways of keeping flocks away from fields of ripening wheat. He found large numbers of Galahs were dying, so he collected some and stored them in his refrigerator, along with the food, and sent several off for analysis. The reply came back a few days later with the news that they had died from psittacosis, a disease that can affect humans. We decided we should eat out.

The Galah is one species that has benefited from the practices of the agricultural and pastoral industries, mainly the provision of watering troughs in grazing areas, but also the introduction of exotic grasses such as wheat. In several cities outside the normal range of Galahs, escaped pets have bred up and formed flocks that visit back yards for handouts. At least some of the birds I saw flying around Perth were feral eastern States Galahs, identifiable by the colour of the skin around the eye. It is probable that they have the same pest potential as any introduced bird, and they are likely contaminants of the genetic integrity of the local population.

More than thirty years ago, I photographed a Galah with its mouth wide open. It looked so comical and so full of its own importance that I put the photograph aside until I could take a complementary one to make a pair. Recently my patience was rewarded, when I snapped a shot of a Galah looking absolutely bored. The two were put together in this painting.

Male Red-tailed Black-Cockatoo

A young artist, Sydney Parkinson, was employed by Joseph Banks to sail with Captain James Cook on his first expedition. At Batavia in January 1771, he died of dysentery on the way home, leaving a journal and many drawings. Among natural history subjects, his portfolios include twenty-nine birds, mainly petrels, but also a female Red-tailed Black-Cockatoo. It was said to have been sketched at Botany Bay, but was more probably made at the Endeavour River in north Queensland. It was the first Australian land bird to be illustrated.

John Latham used the drawing as the basis for his description of the species in 1790, naming it after Joseph Banks. Parkinson's journal was published by his brother Stansfield in 1773, with a portrait of the artist and twenty-seven of his drawings. Unfortunately, distribution of the book was curtailed by Court Order as it pre-empted the official account of the expedition by Dr John Hawkesworth, and it was not re-issued until 1784.

Red-tailed Black-Cockatoos form several discrete populations that, in the past, were described as separate species. I would not be surprised if further study proves that the south-western arboreal form, *naso*, is a distinct species, as it has a differently shaped bill, modified for the extraction of seeds from the "nuts" of the eucalypt known as the Marri. The form in Victoria that feeds mainly on stringybark seeds is now extremely rare and may have to rely on revegetation for survival. My painting of it is a tribute to the artist-grazier Richard Weatherley, who not only has produced one of the best black-cockatoo paintings, but has devised a seeder that makes revegetation rapid and efficient. The background of the painting depicts a denuded landscape with rows of emerging trees planted by Richard's seeder.

Female Red-tailed Black-Cockatoo

Palm Cockatoo

To borrow from George Orwell, "All birds are equal but some are more equal than others". For me, birds of prey are the most equal, followed closely by black-cockatoos. Just why I like them so much is hard to say. They hardly conform to conventional ideas of beauty – indeed, by such criteria the Glossy Black-Cockatoo, with its bulbous beak, is downright ugly, yet the beak is beautifully adapted to the delicate removal of tiny seeds from casuarina nuts. The female is, I think, the only bird in the world with asymmetrical markings.

The Yellow-tailed Black-Cockatoo was originally called the Funereal Cockatoo, in reference to its sombre garb and stately progression through the air. I have painted the Tasmanian form for a very simple reason: it has a pure yellow tail. The large mainland form has a freckled tail that looks great in life but terrible in a painting. Incidentally, it is incredibly difficult to paint yellow in shadow, so the tail on this bird is something of a technical achievement, the result of weeks of experimentation with all manner

of colours. If you doubt me, try it – you will come up with every shade of green until you hit upon the one unlikely ingredient that makes it work.

There is a rule in biology, known as Bergmann's Principle, which states that individuals within a species are larger at high latitudes than those at lower latitudes. According to this principle, Yellow-tailed Black-Cockatoos from Tasmania, western Victoria and South Australia (race *xanthonotus*, which means yellow-eared) should be larger than more northerly birds (race *funereus*, meaning funereal). Such is not the case, so perhaps it is just another exception to a not entirely universal rule. There is, however, the possibility that the Yellow-eared race may actually be a separate species. The ramifications are fascinating, because there are two similar black-cockatoos in south-western Western Australia, short-billed and long-billed, either of which could be the same species as either of the two eastern Yellow-tails. As a whole, the black-cockatoos represent an interesting and exciting group for study.

Purple-crowned Lorikeet

Varied Lorikeet

I never look at a Varied Lorikeet without thinking of that fragile genius, Edward Lear, who illustrated and named this species in his marvellous book, *Illustrations of the Family of Psittacidae or Parrots*. The book, begun in 1825 when Lear was still a teenager, contains some of the most remarkable paintings of parrots ever produced, and his innovative handling of the lithographic medium influenced every great natural history book for the rest of the century. Varied Lorikeets have something of the look of Edward Lear – myopic and slightly comical. One can almost imagine them sitting in bloodwood trees composing limericks, just as Lear entertained the children of the Earl of Derby with whimsical ditties, laying the foundations for his later fame. But he was an even greater artist than he was nonsense poet, a fact appreciated by John Gould who exploited the young man to the extent that Lear's health broke down at the early age of twenty-six, with the tragic result that he never painted birds again.

The Varied Lorikeet occupies the tropical woodlands from about Broome, Western Australia, to the inland foothills of the Great Dividing Range in Queensland. It is very much a nomadic species, depending on flowering eucalypts, bauhinias and grevilleas for sustenance. I noticed a pair entering a hollow in a woollybut tree near Derby, and, thinking they had a nest, erected a hide on a dead limb about 15 metres (50 feet) up. It turned out that it was a roosting hollow, and they returned only after sunset, as I found after sitting in the hide all day. When I went out the following morning, the limb I had been sitting on had fallen down and lay shattered at the base of the tree.

The Purple-crowned Lorikeet, while physically no smaller than its relatives, always looks more fragile to me, due to its unusual colouring. Its wings are quite small in area compared to the body, so it must fly very fast just to stay aloft, and hits a perch at some speed, indicating good shock absorbers.

Eclectus Parrot

erdinand Bauer, an artist sailing with Captain Matthew Flinders on his historic circumnavigation of Australia in 1802–3 aboard HMS *Investigator*, made the first, and by no means least, painting of the bird now known as the Australian Ringneck. It varies considerably in plumage over its range and different populations have in the past been considered different species, with vernacular names such as Port Lincoln Parrot, Twenty-eight Parrot, Cloncurry Parrot, Mallee Ringneck, Barnard's Parrot and Bauer's Parrot.

The form that Bauer painted was the Port Lincoln, collected probably in the region of Spencer Gulf, South Australia, by the expedition's naturalist, Robert Brown. The specimen was later described scientifically by Coenraad Temminck who gave it the name *Platycercus baueri*. Unfortunately, the parrot had already been described scientifically as *Platycercus zonarius*, so Bauer missed the honour of having a bird species named after him. However, the illustration he did of the parrot, as well as his other magnificent paintings of Australian flora and fauna, are an even greater memorial.

The Eclectus Parrot has a very restricted range in Australia, being found in rainforests from the Pascoe River to Massey Creek on eastern Cape York Peninsula. Occasional sightings further south could be aviary escapees, but may represent a hitherto unrecorded nomadic habit. The scarlet and blue female is more brilliantly coloured than the predominantly green male. Usually they congregate in small groups, feeding mainly on fruits and blossoms. In the breeding season, as many as eight birds have been observed attending a single nest.

Regent Parrot

iesse's dam was a special place for me when I was very young. It was out of bounds, but I used to sneak through the fence whenever I could and dart over the dam wall, hoping to remain undetected. I spent endless hours there, trying to catch tortoises and gilgies, or following Black-fronted Dotterels around the water's edge.

I remember best a dead wattle tree on the dam wall and the flock of Regent Parrots that perched there at odd times. We called them "smokers" then. They appeared mysteriously and silently – always while I was looking elsewhere. When I looked back, there they would be, sitting upright among the dead twigs. I had a peculiar longing, almost like a fever, to get closer, something I hadn't felt with other birds. I would try to creep up, and usually got close enough

to see the red patches on their wings before they took off as silently as they came, but it was never close enough. It never occurred to me that they were wanting to drink, and if I had sat quietly at the water's edge they would probably have landed all around me.

Regents in south-western Australia are said to be duller in plumage than south-eastern birds, but the brightest bird I ever saw, shown in the painting above, was between Doodlakine and Bruce Rock in the West many years ago. At about the same time, Joseph Forshaw, the parrot expert, has told me he saw a similarly beautiful bird at Kojonup. In those days, Regents were common, but since then have declined, possibly due to competition with Galahs for the ever-decreasing supply of nest hollows.

Princess Parrot

Bourke's Parrot

The Princess Parrot is, to me, the most elegant of Australian birds. I described it in an earlier book as the epitome of the inland, its colours and form in complete harmony with its harsh environment. Because of its beauty, the Princess Parrot is a popular cage-bird and there are many more in captivity than there are in the wild. Breeders of cage-birds are always on the lookout for colour mutations, and nurture them when they occur. To me, very few look as good as the original stock, or "wild-type". However, one mutation of the Princess is extremely beautiful, resulting from the loss of lipochrome (or yellow colouring) from its plumage, so, instead of being basically olive in colour, it is blue. I remember seeing a bird vaguely similar to this in the wild north of Kalgoorlie at Hughie's Find (Hughie is pronounced "Yewie") in 1949 or 1950, one of a small group we flushed from the ground. I can still see their tails waggling from side to side as they took off. Nowadays it requires really dedicated efforts to see Princess Parrots in the wild, but they are there, mainly in the western deserts, where the best opportunity for a sighting is along the Canning Stock Route.

Major Thomas Mitchell, the explorer, was not the first to find Major Mitchell's Cockatoo, but he did discover Bourke's Parrot which came to his notice on the Bogan River in western New South Wales. In his book "*Three Expeditions…*" he named the new bird after the Governor of New South Wales, Major-General Sir Richard Bourke, and this name was perpetuated by John Gould in his official description published in 1841. Elizabeth Gould's lithograph of a pair of Bourke's at their nest-hole, inspired by Mitchell's specimens, was completed shortly before her untimely death following childbirth. The beautiful pink colouring she mixed for the birds has subsequently faded in many of the 250 hand-coloured prints, particularly in those examples ripped mercilessly from the pages of the Goulds' book *Birds of Australia* and subjected to ultra-violet light on lounge room walls.

Red-winged Parrot

Some years ago there was a commendable attempt to rationalise the common names of Australian birds. One rather pedantic objection was to the use of names such as Princess Parrot and King Parrot on the grounds that these are titles and not applicable to birds. Another more logical proposal was to apostrophise names of birds honouring people's names, so Lewin Honeyeater became Lewin's Honeyeater and Bourke Parrot became Bourke's Parrot. I suggested, without success, that the Australian King-Parrot should be King's Parrot, as it was named after Governor Philip King, who was Australia's third Governor from 1800 to 1806. At the time I could not find relevant evidence, but have since uncovered sufficient proof – too late. Firstly, two Frenchmen, R.P. Lesson and Dumont D'Urville, from the ship *La Coquille*, published an account of a trip to Bathurst in 1824. Included was a discussion of birds found at Port Macquarie: "The King's Parrot (*Platycercus scapulatus*, Vigors) or,

The Parakeet of King, a former Governor of New South Wales". Secondly, some birds sent from New South Wales by Governor King were discussed at a meeting of the Zoological Club of the Linnaean Society in 1825. An account of the discussion concluded: "the well-known species of Parrot, the *Platycercus scapulatus*, commonly called the King Parrot was also originally called King's Parrot". The reason for the name was, I believe, because Governor King's dress uniform was scarlet and green, the colours of the parrot.

The other bird illustrated here was originally described as two species: the Red-winged Parrot in the east and the Crimson-winged Parrot in the north. As early as 1900 it was realised that the two were conspecific and jointly were given the name Red-winged Parrot. It is interesting to note that northern birds are still popularly called Crimsonwings, indicating how long a name can persist after being officially rescinded.

Northern Rosella

I do my paintings on an old tilting drafting table in a studio attached to our home. Facing me is a large window overlooking a wild tangle we call a garden where I can see Pale-headed Rosellas coming to the seed we put out for them. They nest here, unless the local possums are using their nest hollow. They visit the nest hollow every day of the year whether they are using it or not, pressing the fleshy cere above their beaks onto the wood around the entrance. Are they testing temperature and humidity, or listening for termites? I have no idea. At least six birds visit our place – they fight often, flying up into the air with tails spread. No two are exactly alike. The left-hand bird in the painting has a distinct cream bib. When it was immature, this area as well as its head were mealy red, indicating some genetic affinity with Eastern Rosellas – which occur about one hundred kilometres to the south. Most of the young rosellas here have some red feathers on the head, and occasional adults have a red fleck or two. Because there is a narrow hybrid zone between Eastern and Pale-headed Rosellas, they are considered to be races of one species, but as they are well on the way to achieving specific status, and are very different in appearance, it is sensible to retain separate common names for them. In the wild, the Northern Rosella does not come into contact with the Pale-headed Rosella, but in captivity the two readily hybridise, so they are also considered to be conspecific. Many Northern Rosellas have a "smudged" look, resulting in the aviculturalists' name, Smutty Rosella.

Pale-headed Rosella

Immature Crimson Rosella, Lamington National Park

Adelaide Rosella

Adult Crimson Rosella

The Crimson Rosella and its offshoots, the Yellow and Adelaide Rosellas, are good examples of Gloger's Rule, an ecological principle which states that races in dry climates are less heavily pigmented than races in humid climates. The Crimson Rosella inhabits wet forests in eastern Australia, and is heavily pigmented, while the lightly pigmented Yellow Rosella lives in the dry river forests of the Murray-Darling valley. The Adelaide Rosella is a "hybrid" between the two and varies from mainly yellow in the dry north to mainly red in the more humid south. I came across the Adelaide Rosella shown here south of Adelaide – it is very close in pigmentation to the Crimson Rosella and is one of the most beautiful parrots I have seen.

The painting of the Crimson Rosella (top left) is of a young female from Lamington National Park in the Macpherson Range in southern Queensland. Because I saw it being fed by a fully coloured male, I assumed it was a juvenile, but an expert I consulted suggested it was a sub-adult bird mated to an adult. Male parrots regularly feed their mates. Anyhow, I painted it because it seemed more attractive than the adults.

Paradise Parrot

Mulga Parrot

A number of Australian birds have become extinct in the past two hundred years: Tasmanian Emu, King Island Emu, Kangaroo Island Emu and Western Rufous Bristlebird. The Paradise Parrot, once described as "the most beautiful paroquet that exists", has not been "reliably" reported since 1927 and there must be considerable doubt that it does still exist except in museum drawers. I receive more queries about Paradise Parrots than any other bird, mainly from people who believe it could still be found with a bit of luck, but also occasionally from those who have "reliably" seen it. One told me he had seen, from his car window on the one trip, a Paradise Parrot and a Night Parrot (at that time also believed to be extinct). "Amazing!" I said. Some of my more cynical friends believe that the periodic rumours of definite sightings originate with unscrupulous cage-bird breeders who hybridise Mulga and Golden-shouldered Parrots and try to pass off the progeny as Paradise Parrots, hoping for enormous prices. I am not so cynical and haven't given up hope that a few genuine birds still exist, but if I found any I certainly would not tell anyone.

Rainforest Birds

Rainforests in Australia are relatively small in area but huge in terms of the wildlife occupying them. One study suggests that the remaining mainland rainforests could be contained in a circle measuring 70.6 kilometres in diameter, and the Tasmanian rainforests in a circle 38.1 kilometres in diameter. Yet these areas are thought to contain about half of Australia's species of terrestrial fauna and flora. Approximately one hundred and fifty species of birds regularly occur in rainforest, and about sixty of those are confined to it.

Different rainforest birds exploit different layers of the forest. Ground-feeders include cassowaries, pittas, thrushes, fern-wrens, lyrebirds and logrunners; shrub-feeders include scrub-wrens, fairy-wrens and robins; mid-storey-feeders include whistlers, shrike-thrushes, flycatchers, warblers and riflebirds; and canopy-feeders include pigeons, cuckoo-shrikes, honeyeaters and orioles. Because of the ready availability of food, rainforest birds occur in large numbers, yet, due to the abundant vegetation, are rather difficult to see. The birds themselves have the same problem, so have developed loud voices to announce their whereabouts. Those with the loudest voices are the Manucode, which has a coiled windpipe, the riflebirds and the Tooth-billed Bowerbird. I sat in a hide near a bower of the latter bird, and its owner perched above me for an hour, calling at maximum decibels the whole time. Five minutes into its performance I developed a monumental headache and by the time the bird flew off I was paralysed by reverberating eardrums. My favourite bird call is that uttered by the Rose Robin. It has a sepulchral, haunting quality, which, although not loud, carries for a long way. The catbirds have the most easily recognisable calls, sounding like querulous cats, but also have an often-heard but seldom-recognised mechanical click. Albert's Lyrebird is just as accomplished a mimic as its better known relative the Superb Lyrebird, but the lyre feathers of the males are quite different. I picked up a lyre feather from an Albert's Lyrebird in the Macpherson Range and have since shown it to some of Australia's best birdwatchers. Not one has been able to identify it correctly.

Most rainforest birds breed in the rainy season. There is a high predation on nests by reptiles and mammals, so many pairs make several attempts before successfully raising a brood. All sorts of strategies are employed to protect nests. Riflebirds drape snake skins around the circumferences of their nests, while robins and flycatchers build in slender saplings, often with prickly trunks. The Fairy Warbler invariably builds near a stinging wasps' nest, and fruit-doves build in the outer twigs of flimsy horizontal branches. Mistletoebirds drape their dainty nests with the droppings of spiny caterpillars to simulate the webs of those distasteful insects.

Once eggs are laid they may be incubated rapidly, and the chicks develop quickly, to minimise the time spent in vulnerable nests. The fruit-doves grow wing feathers quickly and are able to leave the nest before being fully fledged. Several cuckoos inhabit rainforests, but only one, the Chestnut-breasted, is confined to them. It is migratory, like many other rainforest birds such as pittas, flycatchers and kingfishers. These birds arrive and depart via Cape York in waves. For several days one sees Red-bellied Pittas, then a few days of Black-faced Monarchs and so on. They may move at night as well as by day, because some are picked up dead after hitting windows during the night. I identified many rainforest species, principally fantails, from feathers found at a Ghost Bat's roost, obviously captured in transit at night.

Any discussion of rainforests invariably concludes with a plea for increased conservation. I add my voice on behalf of the sixty bird species that cannot exist without adequate forests and whose continued survival depends on our protection. Their demise would only foreshadow our own.

Lovely Fairy-wren

83

Pale-yellow Robin

Grey-headed Robin

I t was natural for the earliest European settlers in Australia to use familiar names for the birds they encountered. A plump, confiding little bird with a red breast reminded them of the robin "back home", so robin it became. But research has shown that despite the superficial similarity, Australian robins are not even remotely related to the European species, and are more closely allied to crows and crow-like birds. If so, then one of the most beautiful of them must be the male Pink Robin, a denizen of forests in south-eastern Australia and Tasmania. In my picture I have tried to recreate a most beautiful scene I saw in a Tasmanian beech forest. These ancient trees have existed there, and on the highlands further north, since Australia broke away from Antarctica long ago. In the background I have shown some falling trees, reminding us how precious they are and how imperative is their protection.

A number of other robins also inhabit rainforest – including the equally beautiful Rose Robin, and the panda-like White-faced Robin, the Grey-headed Robin and the Eastern Yellow Robin. The other painting shows the least obtrusive of them, the Pale-yellow Robin. It is quite common but usually overlooked, because it is economical in its movements, its calls are discreet, and its plumage, similar in male and female, harmonises well with the foliage of the understorey. Nevertheless it has a quiet beauty of its own. The bird I have shown is from the MacPherson Range in southern Queensland – further north birds have a pale russet wash over the face.

Pink Robin

Rose Robin

Fairy Gerygone

Rufous Fantail

The Rose Robin in Queensland spends summer in highland rainforest, where it breeds, and winter at lower altitudes in eucalypt forest. As well, many birds from the south-east come up for winter. In my favourite patch of woodland in the Moggill State Forest, near our home, dozens of robins spend the cold months. They are not particularly obvious, but they do have a distinctive little call-note, a rather nasal "chick", which reveals many more in the bush than one sees. In the first week or two of August, the males burst forth into their beautiful, introspective song, and by mid-August all have gone, back up into the mountains or down south to breed. The nest is one of the most aesthetically pleasing artefacts of nature, decorated with mosses and lichens to match the surroundings. One that I saw in a lichen-covered stinging tree, on Duck Creek Road in the Macpherson Range, was, with its attendant owners, the most beautiful sight I have ever seen. I was unable to locate the painting I made of it, so have included here another nest, which I found at O'Reilly's in the Lamington National Park.

For many years, three Rose Robins wintered in our garden, but we haven't seen them since Noisy Miners took up residence. Each year, Rufous Fantails pass through while on migration, spending several days in our garden before moving on. Like the Rose Robin, they have a distinctive call-note that alerts us to their presence, but it is much higher-pitched, almost at the limit of human hearing. During summer, they are among the commonest birds in rainforests, usually seen flitting erratically through under-storey shrubs or sitting on the ground in a patch of sunlight.

Victoria's Riflebird

Paradise Riflebird

Various derivations have been cited as the origin of the unusual name "riflebird". Most convincing is that given by R.P. Lesson, senior medical officer aboard the French vessel *La Coquille* which visited Sydney early in 1824. Lesson collected birds on trips to Bathurst and Port Macquarie, where he obtained the Paradise Riflebird, about which he wrote: "This is commonly called the Rifleman in Sydney, from the name of a soldier who killed six or seven of them on a journey to the interior of the country". Riflebirds have a puff of feathers at the base of the bill, and in some early accounts they were referred to as "Ruffle-Bills" which could have changed via "Ruffle-Bird" to "Riflebird". I recall reading somewhere that the blue and green iridescent colours were reminiscent of those worn by a rifle regiment, but cannot now trace the reference.

I have been lucky enough to witness the remarkable courtship displays of all three Australian species, but not in enough detail to attempt a painting. The male chooses a display perch where he is seen to best advantage by the female, not necessarily by someone wanting to paint him. Until I have better luck, here are some males in more mundane poses. One aspect of the riflebirds that cannot be shown visually is the lovely rustling sound made by the wings in flight, rather like the belle of the ball descending a staircase in her taffeta grown. The female riflebirds rustle in flight also, although they have differently shaped wing feathers. Their bills, which look longer than those of the males, are used for digging into rotting wood.

Magnificent Riflebird

Red-bellied Pitta

Rainbow Pitta

Birdwatchers arriving from overseas who contact me usually have a list of birds they want to see. Pittas are invariably high on the list, being colourful birds confined to rainforests where they are not always easy to see even though fairly common. Some people see them frequently; others have great difficulty. My advice to the latter is to look through intervening vegetation to the ground thirty to forty metres ahead, watching for stop-start movement, and not to forget that although they are ground birds, pittas also perch in trees.

On a visit to Darwin some years ago, I was anxious to find a Rainbow Pitta's nest, having heard that they are very difficult to locate. Johnny Estbergs, whom I taught many years ago in Katanning in Western Australia, and Tony Hertzog took me out to a spot near Fogg Dam where they thought we would have a good chance. We pulled up near a plantation of pine trees about one hundred metres from a likely patch of rainforest. I glanced into the pines and, seeing a heap of twigs about ten metres up, said jokingly "a pitta's nest". Lifting my binoculars to examine the twigs, I was absolutely astonished to see a pitta fly out. What it was doing nesting so far outside its normal habitat I have no idea. We went down into the rainforest and in the next two hours found thirteen nests. I sat quietly near one and had the best views I have ever had of pittas as the pair fossicked around looking for worms and feeding their young. Perhaps I should invite Tony and Johnny to come looking for Paradise Parrots.

Yellow-billed Kingfisher

When I was quite young, my aunt, Mavis Yates, gave me a book which contained a reproduction of Henry Constantine Richter's beautiful lithograph of Buff-breasted Paradise-Kingfishers from Gould's supplement to *The Birds of Australia*. It made such an impression on me that, when the opportunity arose, the Slater family moved from Western Australia to Innisfail in north Queensland where the kingfisher was common and I was able to study it at close range. It certainly lived up to my expectations.

The first specimens of the species, used by Richter as models, were collected by John Macgillivray, a naturalist from HMS *Rattlesnake*, at Evans Bay on Cape York Peninsula late in 1849. He also collected the other Australian rainforest kingfisher, the Yellow-billed, at Evans Bay. I first came across the Yellow-billed in the Lockerbie scrub at the tip of Cape York, when we played a tape of a Chestnut-breasted Cuckoo's call. Much to my surprise, as well as a cuckoo, a kingfisher came bustling up, crest erect, but

I soon found that the trilling calls of both species are rather similar, with the cuckoo's more truncated. In life I doubt that the two species ever confuse each other, but a recording has sufficient distortion to trigger an interspecific response. We found five Yellow-billed Kingfishers' nests in a short space of time, tunnelled into arboreal termite mounds. Four of them were just outside the rainforest, so it would seem that this kingfisher favours forest edges.

The paradise-kingfisher is more adapted to the forest interior, and favours terrestrial termite mounds for its nest. In the Lockerbie scrub it is very common and we found many nests. Being so low, the nests are often raided by goannas, and one of our party actually saw a goanna take an adult kingfisher from its nesting chamber. We found one nest ideal for photography, but when we went back to set up a hide, found only a handful of feathers scattered about, including the beautiful long central tail-feathers. I wore one in my hat for a long time, but eventually it proved irresistible to some dirty rotten thief.

Rose-crowned Fruit-Dove

The Banded Fruit-Dove is a rainforest bird that lives in a restricted environment confined to the western edge of the Arnhem Land escarpment in northern Australia. In the desiccated sandstone gullies are restricted monsoon forests, remnants of a more humid past, which provide much of the pigeon's sustenance and shelter. However, growing in fissures in the sandstone cliff faces are solitary Rock-Figs, natural bonsai plants, that provide a favourite source of food. During the fruiting season, May–August, the doves periodically leave their sheltered gullies to clamber among the fig-tree branches seeking ripe fruit. I have recreated opposite a magnificent view I had in Kakadu National Park of a male dove at Yurmikmik Gorge which impressed me as much with its parrot-like climbing ability and enormous gape as by its dignified beauty.

I was lucky enough to have excellent views also of the Rose-crowned Fruit-Dove among the mangroves at the northernmost tip of Cape York. Normally, it occupies the upper canopy of the rainforest and the best one can hope for are fleeting glimpses or silhouettes. However, at Cape York many were nesting in the mangroves, usually on a low flimsy branch overhanging a waterway, so our boat could be manoeuvred into a good position for perfect viewing. The painting gives a rough idea of what we saw.

Both of these pigeons, and others like them, have a narrow "whistle-tip" to the outermost primary wing feather, which causes a distinctive whistling sound in flight. It is most frustrating in rainforest to hear the whistling in the dense canopy without catching a glimpse of the instigator.

Water Birds

Although Australia has been described as the driest continent, with two-thirds of its area being waterless for much of the time, a large proportion of its birds spend their lives on or near water. Most of the Australian wetlands are ephemeral, alternating between flood and drought, particularly in the inland. Many species of water birds are adapted to a nomadic existence, searching out new lakes or swamps as others dry up, sometimes moving long distances.

When I lived at a railway settlement on the edge of the waterless Nullarbor Plain, I often recorded ducks and grebes that landed on the silver-painted roofs on moonlit nights, having mistaken them for water. On one occasion when I was following an old bush track in the Gibson desert, it started to rain for the first time for many months and overnight several puddles formed. Imagine my surprise next morning when I saw two Grey Teal dabbling in the small pools. They were only two of what is probably a steady stream of ducks and other birds flying at night looking for water. Whenever an inland claypan or lake fills, within a short time it attracts a population of birds feeding on the explosion of life that water triggers. I remember in particular one recently filled lake which had an old wire fence running across the centre. Towards evening, thousands of Whiskered Terns arrived and settled onto the wires to rest for the night.

Often the birds will breed while the good conditions last, sometimes in extensive colonies. Banded Stilts in particular epitomise this seemingly miraculous adaptation to a harsh and unforgiving environment. They congregate in large flocks on inland salt lakes, feeding on brine shrimp. If conditions are precisely right, they breed on islands in the lake, otherwise they move on as the brine shrimp die off. How do they find another lake? They are not strong fliers, yet must on occasions move long distances – do they fly in one compact flock or scatter individually in all directions? If they scatter, how do they communicate their good fortune when another suitable lake is found? Perhaps there is a pattern of inundation we are not aware of, but which the stilts know instinctively. When the inland dries out, they return to the coast to wait, sometimes for five years or even longer, until their incredibly fine-tuned sensitivities tell them that the lakes are filling again. To the stilts, what we regard as an arid land must be a benign place with a periodic supply of brine shrimp, otherwise they would have died out long ago, as did the flamingoes that once graced the Lake Eyre basin.

Many of Australia's water birds are able to drink salt water and have a special gland like an extra kidney that extracts salt from their blood. The gland is situated at the base of the beak, and a concentrated saline solution can be seen dripping from the bill-tip. One bird that frequents fresh water is the Red-kneed Dotterel, and dissection has shown that it lacks a salt gland. However, I photographed a pair nesting on a salt lake and noticed on their bill-tips drops of moisture similar to those of salt-excreting species.

An important feature of Australia's wetlands is the periodic inundation of marshes flanking the larger rivers. When these rivers flood, vast areas are covered with water, and birds flock in to breed, birds such as egrets, herons, spoonbills and ibis, as well as ducks, including the rare Freckled Duck. The most popular nesting site is lignum, a leafless bush that grows in impenetrable stands where the flood-waters lie longest, but trees such as paperbarks also become covered with nests, particularly those of cormorants and darters.

Closer to the coast more permanent waterways support an enormous population of birds – for instance, in summer there may be as many as half a million ducks in Victoria alone, and probably as many gallinules such as swamphens, coots, moorhens and rails. In dry seasons, the concentration becomes intense and outbreaks of botulism may occur, decimating populations, but such is the nature of adaptation to the Australian environment that in good seasons birds breed up in large numbers to replenish stocks. However, there is an overall decline in many species, due to drainage, salination and disruption to river flow caused by dams and excessive irrigation, as well as by the choking of waterways by introduced weeds such as salvinia and water hyacinth. On the other hand, a few birds such as the Maned Duck and White-faced Heron have proliferated due to the provision of farm dams.

Banded Stilt

MUSK DUCK

PACIFIC BLACK DUCK

WHITE-BROWED CRAKE

PACIFIC GOLDEN PLOVER

COMB-CRESTED JACANA

White-bellied Sea-Eagle attacking Intermediate Egret

Egrets, looking rather attenuated, should, in theory, be anything but aesthetically pleasing. However, they are so graceful I doubt if they could ever look anything but magnificent. In fact, having spent so much time watching egrets I find human ballet distinctly graceless. To see egrets at their best one needs access to a breeding colony early in the breeding cycle, preferably before eggs are laid. Then the delicate plumes are extended in full array, and the heronry takes on the aspect of dozens of brides competitively flaunting their veils.

Egrets come in different sizes, which enables several species to feed in the same ponds without depleting each other's preferred food. The Cattle Egret is a latecomer to Australia, having arrived just before World War II. It feeds mainly on dry land, on insects disturbed by grazing mammals. It is somewhat thick-necked and not as attractive as the others. The Great Egret occurs over much of the world, but there is some suspicion that the Australian population may represent a separate species due to some differences in displays. My painting on pages 20–21 shows one such display, typically aimed at a rival intruding into a feeding territory, not performed by Great Egrets outside Australia. The painting is based on a series of photographs taken by my son Raoul. While the display is unique, what inspired me was the storm-enhanced light shining through translucent wings and tail.

Pied Heron

The Pied Heron was discovered by John Gilbert while he was camped at Moormal, near Port Essington, Northern Territory, in 1841, where he also collected the first specimens of the Green Pygmy-Goose. At the time he wrote a letter in which he expressed the fear he had of Aborigines in Western Australia and stated that he was less fearful at Port Essington, where they seemed more friendly. He was probably unaware that John Lort Stokes from HMS *Beagle* had been speared nearby, two years earlier, while ashore collecting birds with Dr Benjamin Bynoe at the mouth of the Victoria River. Stokes later wrote, " I was … stretched on the poop cabin table, under the care of Mr Bynoe, who on probing the wound gave me a cheering hope of its not proving fatal. The anxiety with which I watched his countenance and listened to the words of life and death, the reader may imagine, but I cannot attempt to describe". In 1846, John Macgillivray and Lieutenant John Ince camped at Moormal to collect birds. Macgillivray later wrote "here it was that poor Gilbert discovered the [Green Pygmy-Goose]". The reference to "poor Gilbert" concerned the fact that

his fears were finally realised on Cape York Peninsula, where he was fatally speared on the 28th of June, 1845. At Moormal, Ince also collected Pied Herons, which he gave to John Gould to illustrate for *The Birds of Australia*.

Nowadays the settlement at Port Essington no longer exists, but one need go no further than the rubbish tip at its replacement, Darwin, to find Pied Herons. It is an incredible sight to see hundreds of these dainty and pristine birds grubbing through the rubbish with Black Kites and crows. They look far better at Fogg Dam, fifty kilometres to the east, where we have spent a lot of time watching them. One particular feature I noticed on a shallow pond where dozens were feeding was the way they flew close to the surface and trailed their feet in the water. All birds participated to such an extent that I concluded it must be a method of bringing fish to the surface. Most of the herons were fishing on the wing, plunging the head downwards into the water as they flew above the surface, an awkward-looking manoeuvre but very productive.

Pied Heron

Little Pied Cormorant

At one stage of our lives, we were inundated by orphaned cormorant chicks to care for. The first one was difficult to feed until I remembered that baby cormorants put their heads inside their parents' mouths for regurgitated fish. Covering the chicks' head with one hand brought an immediate, and very noisy, feeding response, so it was a simple matter to poke a fish down the enormous gape. After that we had no problems – well, not until they started flying. They soon realised that food came via the back door of our home, so sat on the roof just above waiting for someone to appear, whereupon they descended without ceremony, landing with scrabbling claws on head, shoulders and arms indiscriminately. Unfortunately, on one occasion, an unsuspecting visitor, a man of religious probity, very staid and proper, walked out of the door before we could warn him. A string of expletives gleaned from God knows where erupted as he disappeared in a storm of black and white feathers. We have never seen him since. He is still renowned for his saintly demeanour, but I suspect his heavenward gaze is more in anticipation of cormorants than of angels. I was concerned about teaching the young cormorants to fish but need not have worried, as they taught themselves in a nearby river. Each morning they took off, returning, soaking wet, for a feed in the afternoon, then hanging out their wings to dry. Each afternoon they were a little less avid for food, and at last they returned no more, leaving only a fishy aroma that lingered until the next heavy rains.

Little Pied Cormorant

Australasian Shoveler

The word "Shelduck" derives from an old English word meaning "pied". The European Shelduck, to which the name was first applied, and the Radjah Shelduck of northern Australia are conspicuously pied, while the Australian Shelduck, confined to the southern half of the continent, has a more subdued pied appearance in flight, due to large white patches on the wings, more or less hidden while at rest.

When I was seven or eight, I lived in Wagin in the Western Australian wheat belt, and had two friends, both much older. One, a girl, I found particularly glamorous because she had a collection of snakes in bottles of spirit. We built a canoe out of a bent piece of rusty tin from an old roof, sealed it with tar from the road, and wheeled it on a bike to what was probably a dam, but I remember it as a lake, with the idea of catching "Mountain Ducks" as we called the Australian Shelducks. I remember paddling furiously after them. I'm surprised I didn't drown because I couldn't swim – I clearly remember Stanley yelling "bale, bale", at regular intervals.

Whenever we got close they dived, so we never caught any. We thought they had been wounded by duck-shooters because they couldn't fly, but I suspect they were moulting. All ducks except the Magpie-Geese become flightless for a short period while moulting. On reflection, the shelducks were probably young ones because there were about a dozen of them; moulting shelducks usually congregate in huge flocks of up to a thousand birds.

At Katanning, many years later, I went out to a farm to photograph a stone-curlew. The son of the farmer was about two years old, and, while riding his tricycle in the paddock, he flushed a shelduck from her newly hatched brood. The ducklings, stretched in a line, then started following the little boy, who was terrified. The faster he pedalled, his chubby legs pumping, the faster the fluffy baby birds followed him. When his mother rescued him the ducklings settled down around the trike, to be faced with the momentous decision of which to follow once the shelduck returned.

Australian Shelduck

Cotton Pygmy-goose

If one believes in an anthropomorphic God, then one must suspect that He made the Cotton Pygmy-goose to play with in His bath. When I first saw one my instinctive thought was that it wasn't a duck at all but a wind-up toy. Then others swam into view and I had to concede that they were indeed ducks. To them, however, life is too serious to be considered so lightly. Last century they extended in wetlands down the east coast as far as the Hunter River in New South Wales and were described by John Gould in 1865 as "tolerably abundant". Since then, no doubt due to drainage of wetlands and the choking of waterways by salvinia and water hyacinth, their range has diminished, and it is estimated that only 1500 are left. A smaller subspecies, generally known as the Cotton Teal, is still common in South East Asia, so the Australian form does not figure on lists of endangered species. Provided sufficient wetlands in north-eastern Queensland are kept free of introduced water weeds, there is no reason why the Cotton Pygmy-goose should not continue to survive.

The Green Pygmy-goose does not share the toy-duck appearance of the Cotton. It is much darker in colour, thus less obvious in the water. It appears to be more reliant on waterlilies and is rarely seen away from lily-covered ponds and billabongs. Neither of the pygmy-geese has been studied to any great extent, and details of their nesting behaviour are virtually unknown.

Male Green Pygmy-goose

Female Green Pygmy-goose

113

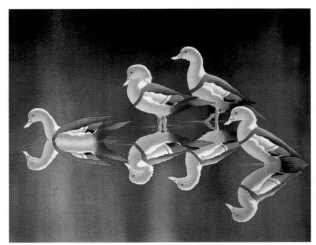

Radjah Shelduck

One hundred and fifty years ago, the Radjah Shelduck ranged from the Richmond River, New South Wales, to the Fitzroy River in Western Australia. Huge numbers were reported on the Burdekin River, Queensland, so it became known as the Burdekin Duck. Nowadays, its range has diminished considerably, with very few records in the Kimberley in the west, or south of about Maryborough, Queensland, in the east. Certainly there are not many now on the Burdekin River, so it is appropriate that the old name of Radjah Shelduck has been resurrected. According to *The Atlas of Australian Birds*, there are no records from the Kimberley since 1900. However, I saw some at the Kimberley Research Station (near Kununurra) in 1955-56, and the painting above recreates a particular sighting, which I have described elsewhere as follows:

"The Burdekin Ducks were observed on a billabong on the Ord River, late in the afternoon. While I was watching, a shot rang out and two of the ducks dropped dead. The shooter had crept up unseen from the other side and must have been almost opposite me because I heard the shot hissing through the grass around me - I clearly remember individual grass-stems slowly toppling. I've often wondered: had he seen the birds lit from behind as I had, would he have been so lacking in soul as to shoot?"

There are still many to be seen in the Top End, even within the city limits of Darwin, where I came across several pairs in January inspecting nesting hollows a considerable way from the nearest water. On the Mary River and in Kakadu National Park they are very tame - we managed to paddle our boat to within a few metres of one small flock, and enjoyed their quiet chittering, almost as if they were gossiping to each other.

Radjah Shelduck

Red-necked Avocet

Black-winged Stilt

There are three Australian representatives of the long-legged family *Recurvirostridae*, which means "upturned bill". Two of them, appropriately known as stilts, have only the slightest upcurve, while the third, the Red-necked Avocet, has a pronounced ski-jump which is more angular in females. Although the beak is so long, the gape is quite small, limiting the size of their prey. All of them feed in the water on small swimming organisms such as brine shrimps, mosquito larvae and water-boatmen. The Black-winged Stilt has the longest legs and obtains all of its food by wading. The Banded Stilt and Avocet have partially webbed toes and frequently swim while feeding, the former often in large flocks. Many years ago, I visited an inland salt lake which was drying up after heavy rains. Out in the centre of the lake I could see a wavering silver line, and could not make out what it was, so started walking forward. Salt-encrusted earth slowly gave way to mud and I plodded on with increasing difficulty, leaving a meandering track of footprints. At last, I could go no further, and raised my binoculars to see thousands of Banded Stilts in an imposing raft, feeding on brine shrimps. I watched them for an hour or so, then, satisfied, turned back. It has not rained in that vicinity since, so I imagine my footprints are still there. The stilts are probably a thousand or so kilometres away, swimming in some other salt lake, a shimmering silver line, part of the mirage of the inland.

Overleaf: Black-winged Stilt

Pacific Gull

Two birds that have introduced themselves into Australia in recent times are the Cattle Egret and the Kelp Gull. Just how quickly they have spread into the environment gives an appreciation of the impact made by other avian immigrants in the more distant past. The first recorded Kelp Gull was collected in Western Australia in 1924, although it lay unrecognised in a museum drawer until it was identified many years later, in 1965, by my friend, the late Julian Ford. The first sighting on the east coast was in 1938 at Port Stephen, New South Wales; in Victoria the first record was in 1953, and a bird turned up in Tasmania two years later. Since then the species has arrived in sufficient numbers to form breeding colonies and now is regularly reported around the southern coastline. Eventually it may come into competition with the local Pacific Gull, which is already decreasing in numbers from unidentified causes.

The painting of the Kelp Gull was conceived on the Huon Estuary in Tasmania; the other picture shows a Pacific Gull dropping a mollusc onto rocks, hoping to break it to reveal the flesh. Pacific Gulls often play with shells and other objects, dropping them and swooping down to catch them in mid-air. Possibly the habit of smashing shells on rocks for food derives from such playful activity.

Kelp Gull

121

Little Kingfisher

The Little Kingfisher is very small, about sparrow size, with a long beak and a virtually non-existent tail. Like the larger and more colourful Azure Kingfisher, it has only three toes on each foot, two directed forwards and one backwards. So dainty is its appearance that I wince every time I see one plummet into the water after a fish or shrimp. However, it invariably survives, and is tough enough to excavate a nesting hole in an earthen bank, termite mound or rotting tree trunk by flying at the chosen site and audibly striking it with the bill. Once the hole is started, the kingfisher works woodpecker-fashion, hollowing out a large chamber. Because it inhabits mangroves along the northern coast and tropical rivers, it is not the easiest bird to see – usually the only glimpse is a flash as it zips low among the mangroves, rapidly alternating between light blue and dark as it moves through dappled sunlight. However, it is not really timid and is best encountered by paddling quietly in a small boat along the mangrove channels. At Fogg Dam, near Darwin, several live in the monsoon forest and presumably fish in the adjacent paperbark swamps. I taught for a short time at a school in north Queensland where one of the pupils gave me a Little Kingfisher that had flown into a window at night. I kept it for a few days in our bathroom, and fed it on shrimps. It had purplish-pink legs, so, despite the fact that the books say they should be black, that's the way I have painted this bird.

Azure Kingfisher

Birds of Prey

Only twenty-four of the world's 300 species of birds of prey inhabit Australia, but between them they patrol all parts of the continent, from rainforest to desert. However, apart from a few obvious species, such as the Nankeen Kestrel, Brown Falcon, Black Kite and Wedge-tailed Eagle, they are not obtrusive in behaviour and are often overlooked. Just how misleading this impression may be was brought home to me when I was given a young Wedge-tailed Eagle to rehabilitate. At that time I was keeping a record of the birds of prey observed flying over our back yard, averaging about seven birds per day. Once it had settled in, the young Wedge-tail started calling loudly every now and then, and I could not find any reason for its discontent until I realised it was reacting to raptors flying over, many of them so high they were almost out of sight. Thus alerted, I rushed outside with binoculars whenever the eagle called, and my daily sightings soared to more than forty. During the three months I kept the bird, nineteen species of birds of prey were recorded, including some such as the Black Falcon, Brahminy Kite, Osprey and Spotted Harrier, that I would otherwise have missed, and indeed would not have believed possible if I had not seen them. Once the eagle went, my daily sightings went down in numbers again to a handful. From this experience, I suspect there is probably a considerable daily passage over most parts of Australia by birds of prey, nature's spy satellites on the lookout for suitable sources of food.

Largest Australian raptor is the Wedge-tailed Eagle, with a wingspan approaching two metres. As with nearly all birds of prey, males are considerably smaller than females. Both are extremely powerful, capable of tackling prey up to the size of small kangaroos. Many individuals, particularly young birds, feed on carrion, but generally older adults take live prey, including rabbits, goannas and birds such as galahs. The Little Eagle is a pocket-sized edition – males weigh less than one kilogram and are the smallest of the world's eagles. At one nest I photographed the male bringing in such elusive, fast-flying quarry as Tree Martins, Elegant Parrots and Ringnecks, indicating its agility in the air.

Goshawks prey principally on birds, which they capture by a quick dash following a stealthy approach. The Grey Goshawk has two colour phases in Australia, one white, the other grey and white. The pure white form in Tasmania was the first Australian bird of prey to be depicted by a European, Georg Forster who sailed with Captain Cook's second expedition. In general, I find it to be a magnificent bird, but I was somewhat disappointed to find that the chicks in a nest I watched were fed on Christmas Beetles.

Three very dissimilar birds of prey are probably closely related with a common ancestor – they are the Square-tailed Kite, Black-breasted Buzzard and Red Goshawk. They probably developed in Australia a long time ago, and each is perfectly adapted to its particular environmental niche. The buzzard has the interesting habit of using stones to break eggs of such ground-nesting birds as emus and bustards, a fact that was well known to Aborigines but only recently observed to the satisfaction of ornithologists.

Fish figure largely in the diet of the Osprey, White-bellied Sea-Eagle and Brahminy Kite. The Osprey, which has a world-wide distribution, is the most spectacular, diving feet-first into the water and often submerging completely. When it emerges, it gives a characteristic shake to remove water from its feathers. The male at a nest I photographed brought in a Long Tom measuring almost one metre, longer than the bird itself. I noticed that it ate the head and left the more succulent flesh for its young. The sea-eagle obviously doesn't like getting its feathers wet, and neatly plucks its prey from the surface. The kite preys in similar fashion, but is just as likely to feed on beach-washed carrion. I photographed one pair at a nest on the well-named Point Torment near Derby, Western Australia and, while succumbing to the hordes of mangrove midges, recorded a writhing sea-snake amongst the items carried in to feed the chicks. Not so far away, I worked at a Whistling Kite's nest, where all but one item of prey I observed consisted of fish. However, this kite's normal fare is terrestrial, ranging from grasshoppers to carrion.

Six species of falcons inhabit Australia, including the spectacular Peregrine, which throughout history has aroused the passions of kings and peasants alike. The aberrant Brown Falcon has a number of colour forms, basically reddish in the inland and brown in more humid areas.

Grey Goshawk (white phase)

JUVENILE PEREGRINE FALCON

AUSTRALIAN HOBBY

Letter-winged Kite

The Black-shouldered and the Letter-winged Kites are the Australian representatives of a widespread group of similar small rodent-eating kites that have developed a habit of hovering in mid-air to search the ground below for their prey. They are just as expert at hovering as kestrels, but have a more clumsy appearance, due to their dangling legs and a tail-heavy look. While kestrels hunt throughout the day, Black-shouldered Kites tend to hunt early in the morning and in the evening, mainly taking mice. The Letter-winged Kite, which under normal circumstances inhabits the Channel Country in Central Australia, is almost entirely nocturnal and its usual prey is the Long-haired Rat. However, the Black-shouldered Kite will also hunt at night, as I found when I arrived at first light to photograph a nest – the crops of the chicks were already bulging with food that could only have been brought in during the previous hour or so of darkness.

The Letter-winged Kite exploits periodic population explosions of the Long-haired Rat, breeding continuously in colonies while the swarms last. Ray Garstone and I camped at a colony on Morney Creek in south-western Queensland, and found some pairs of kites had laid a second clutch of eggs while still feeding just-fledged young from the previous brood. The rats disappear rapidly, forcing many of the kites, probably young ones, to spread out over Australia searching for food. Most probably succumb, but enough survive to replenish numbers during the next rat plague.

Black-shouldered Kite

128

Square-tailed Kite

The Square-tailed Kite has a heavy-lidded look, so it always seems to be half asleep – when its crest is up it reminds me of Velasquez' portrait of Pope Innocent X, with its air of world-weary cynicism. We found one on the ground once, and, thinking it was sick, picked it up and took it home. It was so gentle that it didn't object and became a household pet. We took it out for a fly each afternoon and it followed us through the bush ranging out in a large circle among the tree-tops. On one occasion it took off after a small rabbit and was about to tackle it when a Peregrine Falcon appeared from nowhere and hit the rabbit. The poor kite headed straight back to me and sat huddled on my arm, wondering what had happened. On several occasions it was attracted by Purple-crowned Lorikeets feeding in flowering eucalypts. The lorikeets darted down almost to ground level to pick up maximum speed then dashed away at three or four times the speed of the Kite which had no hope of catching any. Square-tailed Kites in the wild are active predators on nesting birds, particularly honeyeaters. Baby honeyeaters in the nest start squeaking loudly at about 12 days old and I suspect it is the noise that attracts the kite. One would think that such a habit would be eliminated from the honeyeater population by the kites' predations – those that squeaked would attract a kite and those that didn't would survive. However, the kite has a very large territory and only samples a small proportion of the available nests.

The Whistling Kite is nothing like the Square-tailed Kite in behaviour, appearance or gastronomic preference. Where the Square-tail is essentially a predator, the Whistler is an opportunist, feeding on carrion when it is available, as well as insects, small mammals, reptiles and fish. It also harasses other birds to make them drop or disgorge their food. Its loud martial "whistle" is totally out of character, rather like a petty thief singing the Ode to Joy; nevertheless I felt obliged to paint one in the act of whistling.

Whistling Kite
Overleaf: Little Eagle

Wedge-tailed Eagle

I find the Little Eagle (previous pages) the most difficult of Australian birds to draw and paint, and I have yet to see a convincing picture by any artist. The reason is in its squat shape, abnormally large head and legs, and short tail. A drawing which I know to be anatomically accurate just does not look like a Little Eagle, so it must have an indefinable air that defeats delineation. Every species has its own "look" – except the Little Eagle, which has exactly the same "look" as the Northern Hemisphere Booted Eagle, which leads me to the very unscientific belief that they are races of one species. I have a photo of a juvenile Booted Eagle which has been identified as a Little Eagle by everyone I've shown it to. So to do this painting, which is the best I've yet done of a Little Eagle, I relied heavily on a photograph I took many years ago in the Kimberley. I originally showed the bird with its crest up but it looked ridiculous, I so repainted the

head sleeked down. The Wedge-tail is much easier to paint, and is, in fact, a joy because it is so infinitely variable both in plumage and attitude. More than any other bird I know, it visibly expresses its emotions through changes to body shape, which can switch from sleek with serpentine neck to gross and fluffy in an instant. When it fully raises the feathers on its head and neck and looks skyward – watch out!

My painting of the Wedge-tail above is a tribute to the late, great naturalist David Fleay and his eagle "mate" Horatia which he kept for a quarter of a century. A photograph of Horatia when she was young was one of my most treasured possessions, but regrettably was lost in one of the many shifts we made to new birding localities. The Tasmanian Wedge-tailed Eagle, *Aquila audax fleayi*, was named after David, an honour I perceive as the greatest that can be bestowed on any human.

Wedge-tailed Eagle with young Yellow-footed Rock-wallaby

White-bellied Sea-Eagle

We spent several days late in July watching water birds from a houseboat on the Mary River, in the Northern Territory. In great comfort, we puttered along, cameras at the ready. I was particularly entranced by the sea-eagles which had territories along the river. Their huge nests were features of the largest kadjeput paperbarks, and the females were adding green leaves as linings. A few were already sitting, indicating the arrival of eggs, but most perched atop the tallest dead branches waiting for their smaller mates to arrive with a fish or tortoise. On several occasions we saw the males taking fish in most spectacular fashion, inspiring my paintings.

What intrigued me was the way the eagles could see fish in the water where we could see none, often from a distance of a hundred metres or more. For such big birds they are extremely agile, and snatch their prey from the water without getting wet. The males also chase other birds up to the size of brolgas, hoping they will regurgitate their food, in which case it is snatched up before it hits the water.

Juvenile White-bellied Sea-Eagle

White-bellied Sea-Eagle

This painting is an emotional response to a particular piece of music by Franz Schubert, the *Fantasy in F Minor*, one of his last works, written when he knew he was dying. For a period it was played often on classical radio, which I listen to as I paint, and it always impressed me as an anguished cry by the composer against his impending death at the young age of 31. The words I hear in the music are "Why me?" I was doodling on a pad while thinking about this, and the lines turned into a bird of prey screaming defiance at the sky. All of the falcons have this way of expressing their discontent, but the kestrel probably most of all because it is least able to do anything about it. So it seemed a perfect symbol for what I heard in the music.

The background chose itself – in keeping with the bird as well as expressing the tumbled chaos of Schubert's last year. In this setting, the kestrel's outpourings reverberate around its small world, a deserted quarry, just as Schubert's now reverberate around the world. It would have given him solace in his last moment to know that there is no moment now when one or more of his compositions is not being played and appreciated somewhere on Earth.

The kestrel pictured is in juvenile plumage. Its cere and the skin around the eyes were painted originally in pale blue, which is the usual colour for younger juveniles, but the colour was out of harmony with the rest of the picture, so I made the bird older, perhaps ten months, when the soft parts were changing colour to yellow. It looked better but I then had to change the colour of the bird to indicate the wear that takes place in ten months – the plumage becomes more russet and the dark markings lose definition. Having done that, the background looked wrong, so I glazed it with ultramarine, orange and burnt umber. Eventually the whole picture was reworked just to accommodate that tiny change from blue to yellow.

Brown Falcon –
preliminary sketch

The Brown Falcon is of particular interest because it doesn't conform to the usual falcon pattern. It has abnormally long legs indicating a terrestrial habit – I have seen individuals running down grasshoppers during a locust plague. On one occasion I watched one tackling a snake on the ground, using the length of its legs to strike from a safe distance. The commonest method of taking prey is still-hunting, watching from a convenient perch until something moves on the ground, then pouncing down onto it. It also hovers expertly like a kestrel, often at greater heights indicating superior eyesight. It is an expert robber, particularly adept at dispossessing the Black-shouldered Kite or Spotted Harrier of a hard-earned mouse or lizard. With its incredible eyesight it can detect a kite carrying a mouse from well over a kilometre away, and will hasten off in pursuit with round-arm wing-beats. In some areas it hunts like a Goshawk, stealthily flying through the mulga under the canopy, hoping to startle an unwary bird.

Grey Falcon

The Grey Falcon is a genuinely rare bird and has probably always been so, because of its arid inland environment and the enormous territory it requires. Estimates of its numbers, ranging from 250 pairs to 1000 pairs, are impossible to validate because of the difficulty of finding enough pairs to establish a pattern of distribution. There are vast tracts of seemingly suitable country where it does not occur, and other places that look no different where a number will occur in relatively close proximity. Generally, information about known pairs is kept secret because of collectors' demand for eggs. In one locality, we had three pairs under observation in an area of about one hundred square kilometres. None of them was very tame, leaving their nests when we approached and staying away, contrary to the experiences of observers elsewhere and our experiences with other falcon species. From feathers in the nests, we found doves to be the main item of prey, with occasional Flock Pigeons, Galahs, and Cockatiels. We saw Grey Falcons hunting on several occasions and in each instance a vertical stoop was the method, directed at doves at waterholes. On one occasion a falcon hit a dove directly above me knocking it spinning into a bush almost at my feet. The falcon landed, ran into the bush, seized the dove, which was still fluttering, nipped it on the back of the neck and backed out. I could almost have touched it, and I am sure it was unaware of my presence, so intent was it on its prey.

Australian Hobby with Tree Martin

I suppose the Australian Hobby is my favourite bird, and I have painted it more often than any other species. To me it is the very essence of what birds are about – absolute masters of the aerial environment. Because of its aerodynamic shape with long sickle wings it looks faster in the air than it actually is – several times I have seen Stubble Quail and Common Bronzewings that were being chased pull away in level flight. Where the hobby scores most consistently is when it has a height advantage. Many of the large nesting colonies of Fairy Martins and Tree Martins in inland Australia are visited daily by one or more hobbies. I have watched many times and have noted a consistent pattern of attack. The hobby perches in a nearby tree and watches the stream of martins around the nest site. Suddenly its gaze will fix on a particular bird and it takes off, usually effecting a capture. I am sure it has picked out a sick bird, or a young one just out of the nest, for an adult healthy martin is very hard to catch.

On one occasion I was with a group of birdwatchers admiring a bushlark singing its heart out on a dead stump. We all had binoculars trained on it when a hobby dashed up and snatched it before it could take off. I can't imagine how the bushlark had failed to see the approaching raptor – most falcons and hawks fly through the bush accompanied by a chorus of alarm calls that give plenty of warning that danger is on the way. In the west Kimberley we saw a hobby hunting in cooperation with a Pied Butcherbird, chasing a Rufous-throated Honeyeater. Whenever the poor bird flew into a bush it was chased out by the butcherbird, whereupon it was attacked by the hobby. Eventually the hobby won the day, but I am sure there were occasions when the butcherbird scored. However, I think hobbies like dragonflies more than anything else, often eating them in flight. I have watched many individuals hunting for these insects in the evenings until it was too dark for me to see.

Australian Hobby

Peregrine Falcon

I believe that if alien invaders ever conquer the Earth, their reason will not be to dominate, enslave or eat our species or impose on us a better way of life or impart the secrets of the universe, or any of the other scenarios beloved of science fiction writers, but rather to gain access to the Peregrine Falcon. I can't imagine a more perfect creature inhabiting any part of the universe, so once those far-off civilisations hear about it they will board their space crafts and head in our direction. Just to be on the safe side, perhaps we should delete all records of the devastating effect our usage of DDT had on whole populations of Peregrines, but let us never forget its lessons.

It is the quality of its flight, its absolute mastery of the air that attracts so many worshippers to the Peregrine. In my youth, I often wondered whether the Peregrine could outfly the White-throated Needletail, reputedly one of the world's fastest birds. After witnessing an encounter between the two above my own back yard I have no further doubts.

Many years ago I released a Peregrine that had been injured and rehabilitated. Once or twice a week she returned for food and I thought she might be having trouble catching her own food. Then, one sultry evening I saw her flying among a group of Needletails. She absolutely powered around the sky and ran rings around them – I am sure she was playing with them for whenever she caught up with one swift she veered off after another. They went higher and higher until all I could see were specks against the clouds. I had no doubt then that her fitness for survival was complete, and eventually she returned no more.

Barn Owl

I t is probable that the Barn Owl family developed in Australia, since five, and possibly six, of the world's dozen species occur here and another five live on the islands to our north. They feed on small nocturnal mammals, and, as Australia is so rich in species of mice, rats and small rodent-like marsupials, it is natural that they should proliferate here and occupy all habitats from desert grasslands to rainforest. The barn-frequenting species was so successful that it has now spread out over much of the world. In Europe and North America local conditions have acted on the plumage and they are much more brightly-coloured than Australian birds. A friend of mine did a beautiful painting of a pair and submitted it to a juried exhibition in the United States. I warned him that the jury, familiar with their local birds, would think he had got the colours wrong. He sent it anyway and, sure enough, it was rejected, even though, to judge from the catalogue, it was a superior painting to most that were selected.

So my painting will look strange to Northern Hemisphere critics, but I can assure them that is what Australian Barn Owls look like. My other painting is of the Lesser Sooty Owl, which is restricted to rainforests in north-eastern Queensland. I have only seen one close-up, on the Palmerston highway out from Innisfail. Ray Garstone and I had spent an eventful day on the Atherton Tableland, where I ran into a car that was travelling on the wrong side of the road and Ray ran into a Stinging Tree. He is pretty tough but he must have been in agony, and I was in shock. Driving down the highway that night, I became carsick and Ray had to take over, driving one-handed. About half-way down, we saw an owl sitting on the road. Ray stopped the car and I jumped out, crept up, and was eventually able to touch the bird. I will never forget its enormous eyes, which are not exaggerated at all in the painting. In any event, my carsickness was cured so I was able to relieve Ray of the driving and we got home safely.

Crimson Chat

SPINIFEX PIGEON

CINNAMON QUAIL-THRUSH

CHESTNUT-BREASTED
QUAIL-THRUSH

NULLARBOR QUAIL-THRUSH

153

Nullarbor Quail-thrush

Australian Pratincole

Whenever we head west from Brisbane, I can't wait until we reach the sandhill and gibber country the other side of Cooper Creek, where the desert proper begins. There we start seeing the real desert birds, pratincoles, Gibber Chats, Black Falcons, Letter-winged Kites, Flock Pigeons and Australian Dotterels. We usually find a windmill with a turkey's-nest dam, where all the local birds come to drink and bathe, and we camp nearby. We set up just close enough to see what comes in without discouraging the birds from drinking. There is a steady stream of birds throughout the day, but the pratincoles and pigeons come in just on sundown – the pratincoles alight on the dam wall and run down to the water to take a leisurely sip; the pigeons land right at the water's edge and waste no time, sucking up water greedily for two or three seconds – some even land on the dam surface with outstretched wings. Obviously they are vulnerable then to attack by predators, and I have seen their feathers in a Grey Falcon's nest. Out on the stony gibber plains, the pratincoles and Australian Dotterels nest. Their eggs and small chicks are so well camouflaged that they are difficult to find unless a sitting adult has been pin-pointed. As well, the dotterels, if they have time, cover their eggs with soil when danger threatens. They usually keep their backs, which are mottled like the gibbers, to the observer; if only they kept still they would be overlooked entirely.

The desert quail-thrushes prefer stony ground as well, thriving in conditions where one would suspect nothing could live. The Nullarbor Quail-thrush is generally considered to be a subspecies of the Cinnamon Quail-thrush, but has a different "look", so I suspect further research will show the two to be separate.

Budgerigar

Zebra Finch

HMS *Beagle* became famous because of its association with Charles Darwin. What is not so well known is that *Beagle* spent a lot of time in Australian waters, and its officers collected about 140 species of Australian birds, many of them new to science. Surgeon Benjamin Bynoe was perhaps the most active collector, sending specimens to John Gould in England. Among them was the Painted Finch discovered on Depuch Island on or about the 9th of June, 1840. Only one was collected and Gould noted the unusually shaped bill which is longer and more pointed than other finches'. He further wrote: "I regret to say that it no longer graces my collection, having been stolen therefrom, together with some other valuable birds, in the year 1846…". My painting depicts a drying waterhole in the MacDonnell Range west of Alice Springs, where we spent productive time watching Painted Finches and other desert birds coming to drink. At this waterhole, they arrived singly or in pairs; at other places where I have come across Painted Finches they have also been in small numbers. The naturalist Harry Butler once told me he saw about 4000 at a desert waterhole, surely one of the most remarkable sights imaginable. It must have been the only remaining waterhole for kilometres around and probably attracted every finch in the vicinity, reminding one of the vulnerability of desert seed-eaters, which must have regular water.

Yellow Chat

Crimson Chat

I travel into the arid interior as often as I can, and once civilisation is left behind watch for the flash of scarlet or orange that indicates a chat flitting across the road, for wherever the chats congregate other birds abound. Chats have an innate ability to seek out the tracts of the inland that have most benefited from rain — other nomadic birds, woodswallows, Ground Cuckoo-shrikes, Pied and Black Honeyeaters, Budgerigars and hosts of others arrive soon after, nesting in every available niche while the good conditions last. Then they depart with their multitudes of offspring and may not return to that locality for many years.

The painting opposite portrays the most aesthetically pleasing sight I know – an Orange Chat on a blue-bush. The colour contrast of males in such situations is just perfect, and I suppose I have spent more time gazing at such scenes than any other.

The Yellow Chat is rather harder to find. Probably the only places where there are many are on the floodplains of the Ord, Mary and Alligator Rivers in the north. Some live along the bore drains in the central Channel Country, but they require dedicated efforts to locate. I find the brilliant colouring of freshly moulted males almost painful to look at, impossible to paint, but I keep trying.

Orange Chat

Peter Slater's earliest memories are of birds: crows which he described as "like little old men with their hands behind their backs". Since then he has been consumed by a visual hunger for birds, and can watch them for hours and not count the time lost.

He began recording his observations on film at an early age, eventually photographing about 400 species. He has won more than 50 medals in International Salons of Photography, and was made an *Artiste de la Féderation Internationale de l'Art Photographique* in 1964.

Peter took up painting when, following a move to humid north Queensland, much of his photography collection succumbed to mould and

damp, and had to be taken to the local rubbish dump. This change of medium led to his undertaking more than six years' work to compile *The Field Guide to Australian Birds*, recently listed among the top 100 Australian books of the last 50 years. A second field guide was a Slater family collaboration, Peter's wife Pat, a writer, doing much of the research and assisting with the text, and his son Raoul, a physiotherapist and photographer, preparing the species distribution maps. Peter has illustrated many other books with his paintings, including award-winners *Rare and Vanishing Australian Birds*, and *Where Eagles Fly*.

This book includes more than a hundred birds now occurring in Australia, and Peter Slater selected the paintings to illustrate the beauty and diversity of our avifauna. He paints his beloved subjects only after exhaustive observations in the field. For Peter Slater, "the field" can be anywhere in Australia, not least the garden of his home on the outskirts of Brisbane, Queensland. He has lived in out-of-the-way places and travelled Australia from offshore islands to the unforgiving deserts of the Red Centre to observe, sketch and photograph with an uncanny eye for the idiosyncrasy, the minute detail that enlightens and informs the study of birds. The resultant paintings have those special qualities of beauty, light and life.

Acknowledgements
Everyone Peter Slater has spoken to about birds and bird paintings, or spent time with in the bush, has contributed in some way to this book. Among these hundreds of people, he singles out for special mention Ray Garstone, Michael Morcombe, Eric and Del Lindgren, Tony D'Andrea, Peter Trusler, William T. Cooper, Joseph Forshaw, Ray Harris-Ching, P. Brent Harvey, Sally Elmer, Andrew Isles, Greg Postle, John Halse, Mildred Manning (nee Le Souef), Charles McCubbin, Kay Breeden-Williams, Kevin Redmayne, Tony Pridham, Olive Seymour, Dom Serventy, Vincent Serventy, Laurie and Glen Muller, Stan Breeden, Richard Weatherly, Henry Nix, William and Sharyn Richardson, Noelle McCracken, Malcolm Oxenbridge, Mr and Mrs Ray Leggett, Bruce Scott, Kareena Sullivan, Darren Ruck.

In particular, without the enthusiasm, support and faith of Jan and Steve Parish, this book would never have eventuated. Heartfelt thanks are also due to the crew at Steve Parish Publishing. Thanks also to Colette Evans for typing the manuscript.

Pat and Raoul Slater, as always, have given every support to the project.
Peter's mother, Nell, his greatest fan, died on Christmas Eve, 1996: he is saddened that she did not see the finished work, which is dedicated to her memory.

First published by Steve Parish Publishing Pty Ltd, 1997
PO Box 2160, Fortitude Valley BC, Queensland 4006 Australia
© copyright Peter Slater, 1997
ISBN 1 876282 01 0
Printed in Hong Kong
Copy edit by Wynne Webber, Brisbane, Australia
Designed and fully assembled by Steve Parish Publishing, Australia
Colour separations by Steve Parish Publishing, Australia